HERBS WITH EVERYTHING

HERBS
WITH EVERYTHING

How to grow, preserve, and cook them

SHEILA HOWARTH

With drawings by Yvonne Skargon

SPHERE BOOKS LIMITED
30/32 Gray's Inn Road, London WC1X 8JL

This book was designed and produced by
Park and Roche Establishment, Schaan.

First published in Great Britain by
PELHAM BOOKS LTD 1976
© 1976 by Sheila Howarth

Published by Sphere Books 1977

Designed by Ronald Clark
Photography by Roger Phillips
Printed in Great Britain by Jarrold and Sons Ltd., Norwich

CONTENTS

INTRODUCTION

Herbs bring out violent reactions in people as surely as in the foods they touch. The mere mention of them in casual conversation can brand you instantly as a crank.

The herb garden of the ancient Greeks and Romans supplied the household, not only with herbs for the pot, but with cough mixtures, tonics, sweet waters, love potions, insect powder and cosmetics.

Herbs are notoriously various. They can be a cure or a poison; a taste, a smell and a food. They drift constantly through the pages of the Bible and Shakespeare. Lavender bags, herbal teas and medicinal lungwort, liverwort, woundwort ('wort' meaning plant) used in battlefields and hospitals, still have their separate enthusiasts.

This book is concerned with eating them, raw and cooked. As the Book of Proverbs advises: 'Better a dinner of herbs where love is, than a stalled ox and hatred therein.'

In former times, herbs were used as rescue ingredients, to disguise the slightly 'off' or 'high' foods in summer (long before the days of ice boxes), and to improve the taste of salted and preserved food in winter. Now, ironically, herbs are needed to put taste and flavour *into* much mass-produced frozen and processed food.

This book is for cooks, about herbs in cooking . . . for the kitchen shelf, not the coffee table. It gives the most useful everyday *food* herbs; describes their character, the drinks they enhance and the reasons why . . . also those they might ruin. It tells how to use them, when and what to use them with, how and where they are possible, or impossible, to grow; the correct part of the plant to pick, and how to preserve them.

Although the main purpose of the book is to encourage and stimulate the use of fresh herbs—either home-grown or bought—we have nothing against dried herbs, especially those that are your own produce and properly dried. The need for this form of preserving will depend on your climate and ability to keep up a year-round supply of such indispensable annuals as basil, chervil, dill or perennials which die down in winter and reappear in spring, like tarragon, sorrel, mint and chives. If you have no heated greenhouse, these can be kept going with ingenuity on window sills or even in the bathroom.

Ideally, herbs should be grown close to the kitchen door. How many sauces have gone unmade, and dishes unflavoured, because the particular herbs which would have made all the difference between food and a 'taste experience' went out of reach at a given moment? Not just the last-minute sprinkle of parsley, tarragon, dill or basil, but the long-cooking ones which transform stews and stuffings, are missed out. When you have to change your shoes, put on oilskins and risk something curdling or burning on the stove while you are even briefly away, you may well decide that you never did like parsley sauce with broad beans, fish stuffed with fennel and lemon balm, chicken with tarragon, or sorrel in soup.

Unhappily, most kitchens and back doors are habitually occupied by anything which is sometimes needed, but not fit for a permanent place indoors . . . broken toys, muddy boots, gardening handtools, the dog kennel. I know few kitchen doors which fulfil the demanding requirements of most herbs originating in the Mediterranean climate . . . face south, be protected from north and east winds and storms, and on a well-drained slope.

Lack of this idyllic spot need not, however, put off anyone from growing their own herbs to use fresh. If I had only a postage stamp garden, I would give it over entirely to culinary herbs. You can buy fresh flowers and fruit at any time, but not always bunches of fresh herbs. Where space is limited, they can be grown in mixed borders, on kitchen shelves, on balconies, in pots and in window boxes. The hazard of cultivating herbs in a mixed border of perennial plants, is akin to having a nursery school for all ages and behaviour. All need separate attention at different times.

The quantity of herbs to be used in any dish is entirely a matter of personal taste. This will vary with the kind of herb, the food it is to flavour, and the method of cooking. The individual character of each herb depends on its volatile oils. These are trapped in minute glands on the leaves and stems. We chop or pound them in the kitchen to release the aromatic substances. Some herbs let loose their scent more quickly than others, particularly when in contact with heat.

Discretion is essential. You can only reach the perfect balance by experimenting. Be imaginative, try a combination of herbs, but only a pinch of this or that until the taste pleases you for any particular dish. I know many herb addicts, all masculine, whose occasional show-off cooking gets quite out of hand, with every available herb fighting it out in what should have been a subtle and simple dish.

Too much of the more potent herbs, like sage and rosemary, can damage any dish, just as stuffings for meat and poultry must not be overpowered by the robust flavours of marjoram, bay leaves, thyme and lovage. These release their benefits over a long period of cooking and are best in casseroles, soups and stews. More delicate flavoured herbs should be added towards the end of cooking, an omelette or sauce for instance, so that the full bouquet will not be drowned by overcooking.

When dried herbs are to be used, allow about one third of the amount of fresh ones you would usually need, as the flavour is much more highly concentrated.

Wherever and however you get your fresh herbs, let them lead you to want more of them in the food you eat.

Note: Ingredients in the recipes have been set out in the following order, first the Imperial weight or measurement followed in brackets by the Metric and then the American equivalent, i.e. 4oz (100g/½ cup) butter.

HERBS WITH EVERYTHING

ANGELICA

(Angelica archangelica)

An enthusiastic plant which draws attention to itself whenever it is grown. This, alas, narrows the field considerably, for though most decorative, the branching flower stems often become 8–10 feet (2½–3½ metres) high, and the light green lower leaves easily spread 5 feet (1⅔ metres) across.

The leaves are sharply divided and the tiny yellow-green flowers form in rounded heads 4–6 inches (10–15cm) across in the summer. A native of central and northern Europe, it has become naturalised in other parts of the world and can often be found growing wild on river banks.

In old herb gardens created by monks, all parts of the plant were made to pay for their spacious keep. The roots were used in liqueurs and for making medicines, mainly tonics and stomach-easers; the leaves were used in cooking and for 'tisanes'; oil was distracted from the seeds and roots; and the stems and flowers were candied, which is the way the herb is most commonly used these days. The stems, however, can be chopped and added to salads and tea made from fresh or dried leaves is refreshing as well as a help in feverish colds by producing perspiration.

Cultivation

It must have moist and rich soil, well-drained . . . not a bog, and with partial shade. It is a short-lived perennial and for domestic growing is better treated as a biennial. The seed will not germinate unless it is absolutely fresh as it quickly loses its vitality, but once established it can produce almost everabundant colonies of self-sown seedlings. Plants know better than we do the exact degree of ripeness, and when to toss the seed out into the world. Unwanted seedlings are easy to pull up at an early stage, but remember to do this when they are young as you will soon find you have a forest.

11

Preserving

Candied Angelica Method 1. Choose young stems, before the flowers open, cut them into matching lengths of about 4 inches (10cm) and boil until tender. Take them from the water and peel off the outer skin while they are still hot, return them to the water and simmer gently until they become green. Strain and dry, then weight them and allow 1lb (400g) granulated sugar to every 1lb (400g) of angelica. Spread out the stems in a shallow dish and sprinkle with the sugar. Leave for 2 days then boil together in just enough liquid not to let the syrup brown. Take out the stems and add 2oz (50g) of sugar to the remaining syrup. Simmer this then put back the stems for a further 5 minutes simmering. Drain the angelica and dry off on a tray in a cool oven, 300°F, 150°C, Gas Mark 1. Store in airtight jars.

Candied Angelica Method 2. Cut the stems into 5 inch (12·5cm) lengths. Put into a bowl and cover with a sugar syrup made by boiling together 1lb (400g) sugar to 1 pint (500ml) water. Cover with a layer of vine leaves and leave it to steep for 24 hours. Remove the angelica stems, strain the syrup and discard the leaves. Boil up the syrup and pour over the angelica stems and cover once more with vine leaves. Leave for 24 hours then repeat the process once more. Drain the angelica thoroughly and leave to dry in a warm place for 2–3 days. Store in airtight jars.

To dry the leaves. Pick the fresh young leaves in the morning after the dew has dried. Discard any brown or discoloured leaves. Hang the leaves in bunches in a warm, dry place, away from strong sunlight. Leave until the leaves are quite dry—the length of time taken to dry them will depend on the temperature and atmosphere of the drying place. When quite dry crumble into airtight jars and label.

Fish

Baked Whiting with Angelica

4 whiting
salt and freshly milled black pepper
1oz (25g/2 tablespoons) butter
juice of 1 lemon
1 tablespoon chopped angelica leaves

Clean the whiting and remove the heads. Season well with salt and pepper and place in a buttered ovenproof dish. Dot with the butter, pour over the lemon juice and sprinkle with the angelica leaves. Cover and cook in a moderately hot oven, 375°F, 190°C, Gas Mark 5 for 25 minutes. (Serves 4)

Vegetables and Salads

Green Salad with Angelica

4 angelica stalks about 5 inches (12·5cm) long
salt
1 small cos lettuce
½ box mustard and cress

1 small green pepper (capsicum), de-seeded and chopped
4 tablespoons olive oil
2 tablespoons wine vinegar
½ teaspoon French mustard
pinch sugar
freshly milled black pepper
1 tablespoon chopped parsley

Blanch the angelica stems in boiling salted water for 1 minute. Drain and rinse immediately in cold water, then chop finely. Discard the outer leaves of the lettuce, wash and dry well, and tear into small pieces. Put into a salad bowl with the mustard and cress, angelica and pepper (capsicum). Put the oil, vinegar, mustard, sugar, seasoning and parsley into a screw-topped jar. Shake well to mix. Pour over the salad and toss well just before serving. (Serves 4)

Cakes and Desserts

Steamed Mixed Fruit Pudding

2 tablespoons golden syrup
3oz (75g) dried apricots

4oz (100g/½ cup) butter
4oz (100g/½ cup) caster (granulated) sugar
grated zest and juice 1 orange
2 eggs, beaten
3oz (75g/¾ cup) self-raising flour
2oz (50g/⅔ cup) fresh white breadcrumbs
2oz (50g/½ cup) prunes, stoned (pitted) and
 finely chopped
2oz (50g/½ cup) glacé cherries, finely
 chopped
2oz (50g/½ cup) candied angelica, finely
 chopped

Well butter a 1½ pint (750ml/3¾ cup) pudding
basin. Put the golden syrup into the bottom
and lay about 5 of the apricots on top. Chop the
remaining apricots finely. Cream the butter,
sugar and orange zest together until light and
fluffy. Gradually beat in the beaten egg, a
tablespoon at a time, then fold in the sifted flour
and breadcrumbs. Finally fold in the chopped
fruit and orange juice. Spoon into the prepared
basin. Cover with a double layer of foil and
either stand in a saucepan of boiling water or in
a steamer and steam for 2 hours. Turn out and
serve hot with single (light) or whipped cream.
(Serves 4–6)

Cassata

2 eggs, separated
2oz (50g/⅓ cup) icing (confectioners')
 sugar, sifted
2 tablespoons chopped candied angelica
2 tablespoons chopped candied peel
2 tablespoons chopped walnuts
½ pint (250ml/1¼ cups) double (heavy)
 cream, lightly whipped

Beat the egg yolks and half the icing (confectioners') sugar until thick and creamy.
Whisk the egg whites until they form stiff
peaks, then gradually beat in the remaining
sugar, a teaspoon at a time. Gradually whisk in
the egg yolks. Fold in the angelica, peel and
nuts, then fold in the cream. Turn into a
container and freeze for at least 6 hours.
(Serves 4)

Cream Cheese with Angelica

3oz (75g/⅜ cup) caster (granulated) sugar
1lb (400g/2 cups) cream cheese
2–4oz (50–100g/½–1 cup) chopped
 candied angelica
2 egg whites

Beat the sugar into the cheese and stir in the
angelica. Whisk the egg whites until they form

stiff peaks and fold into the cheese. Put into a
large piece of muslin and leave in a cool place
to drain for at least 4 hours. Turn into a serving
dish and serve with fresh cream. (Serves 6)

Stewed Rhubarb

Angelica added to rhubarb gives an unusual
musky flavour and counterbalances any tart-
ness in the fruit.

1lb (400g) rhubarb
1oz (25g) fresh angelica leaves
4oz (100g/½ cup) sugar
peeled zest of ½ lemon
water

Cut the rhubarb into 1 inch (2·5cm) pieces. Put
into a saucepan with the angelica, sugar and
lemon zest and add enough water to just cover
the fruit. Bring slowly to simmering point and
simmer gently until the rhubarb is tender. Allow
to cool, then chill. (Serves 4)

Preserves

Marmalade with Angelica

If you prefer in this recipe you can use fresh,
rather than candied angelica stalks.

3lb (1·2 kilo) Seville oranges
6 pints (3 litres/7½ pints) water
6lb (2·4 kilo/12 cups) granulated sugar
juice of 2 lemons
4oz (100g/1 cup) candied angelica,
 chopped

Wash and dry the fruit and cut it in half.
Squeeze out the juice and put it into a
preserving pan. Put the pips into a piece of
muslin and tie it up. Add to the preserving pan.
Shred the peel fairly finely and put into the pan
with the water. Simmer the mixture gently for at
least 2 hours, stirring from time to time until the
peel is tender and the liquid is reduced by
almost half. Remove the bag of pips from the
pan and squeeze out any liquid from it into the
pan. Add the sugar, lemon juice and angelica.
Stir over a gentle heat until the sugar has
dissolved, then boil rapidly until setting point is
reached (220°F, 104°C). Remove the pan from
the heat and leave the marmalade to cool for
about 10 minutes. Stir well to distribute the
peel and pour into clean hot jars and cover.
Makes about 10lb (4 kilo)

BALM

Lemon Balm
(*Melissa officianalis*)

This is frequently grown in gardens by people who have not the faintest idea of its many uses. It behaves so obligingly they have forgotten why they wanted it in the first place, and let the new shoots come up year after year, for the sake of the strong lemon scent of the leaves, when brushed against or crushed in the hand.

A bushy, hardy perennial, the plants grow to about $2\frac{1}{2}$ feet in a season, with broad, deeply wrinkled and toothed leaves. These have a delightful fresh appearance early in their lives, but rather lose heart when the plant starts to produce messy clusters of insignificant white flowers from late summer onwards. These are appreciated by bees rather than human eyes.

Balm honey used to be more in demand than any other . . . the nectar is particularly strong (Melissa is Greek for bee). Keepers of bees often rub the inside of hives with bunches of the leaves, to keep their passion strictly confined to home, and prevent them from swarming.

The flavour of balm is not as strong as its scent but the leaves can be used fresh or dried in all manner of ways to enhance other flavours and add mystery to a commonplace dish.

The early, fresh leaves are excellent chopped into salads, though they become a little 'chewy' in middle age. When adding to salads you will find you need not add as much vinegar or lemon juice. Stew a few leaves with any fruit for subtle lemony undertones and finely chop and add to vegetables, especially root vegetables, just before serving. Add to stuffings, sausages, sauces, especially for fish, or in any dish where you would usually use lemon thyme. The leaves are not as strong in flavour, but have the advantage of a melting texture, particularly in omelettes.

If there were no other reason for growing balm, a few fresh, torn leaves, added to a pot of China or Indian tea adds a most refreshing zest, which would be demolished by either lemon or milk.

As a drink it was grown and used for other things than mere pleasure. An infusion of the leaves, dried or fresh, helped to bring down high temperatures, was good for the memory, a heart stimulant, sharpened the senses, lifted depression, soothed nervous disorders and was an all-round spirit-raiser—the bees know what they are about! It is also used in pot-pourri.

Cultivation

It is very easy to grow from seed or by divisions of the root and prefers a fairly moist soil in semi-shade, though it will grow without a grumble in any soil or position. This adaptability has led to it being naturalised in all temperate climates, though a native of the warmer south.

Plant at any time from autumn to spring, or sow the seeds in spring. Any left to ripen on the plant will seed themselves, and when particularly pleased with their growing conditions, can become a nuisance. Cut down the stems in the autumn. The root clumps rapidly increase, but, unlike mint are not long distance travellers, and stay in a tight circle which is easy to control by dividing in spring or autumn.

The roots grow very well in a windowbox or tub, and can be left for years with little attention apart from watering and an annual feed, until the roots are too cramped in their containers. When replanting, keep the new outer roots and discard the old centre.

Preserving

Balm does not dry very well but can be frozen. If you only want to store it for up to two months, pack small bunches in polythene bags straight into the freezer. If you want to keep the herb for a longer period, blanch in boiling water for 1 minute, drain, dip in cold water, dry well, pack into polythene bags and freeze.

Sauces and Stuffings

Balm Sauce

This sauce goes particularly well with fish, but can also be served with pork and veal.

1oz (25g/2 tablespoons) butter
1oz (25g/4 tablespoons) flour
½ pint (250ml/1¼ cups) milk
salt and pepper
1 tablespoon chopped balm leaves

Melt the butter in a pan, stir in the flour and cook over a gentle heat for 1 minute. Remove from the heat and gradually stir in the milk. Return to the heat and bring to the boil, stirring all the time. Season to taste with salt and pepper and shortly before serving, stir in the balm leaves. (Serves 4)

Variations: Replace half or all the milk with fish or veal stock.

Balm and Onion Sauce: Chop 2 onions and cook in ¼ pint (125ml/⅝ cup) salted water for 10 minutes. Use this stock in place of ¼ pint (125ml/⅝ cup) milk and continue as the recipe above.

Balm Butter

This, slightly lemon flavoured, butter can be spread on fish, chicken or veal before grilling (broiling).

2oz (50g/¼ cup) butter
freshly milled black pepper
1 tablespoon chopped balm

Cream the butter and beat in the pepper and chopped balm.

15

Savoury Rice and Balm Stuffing

Use this for stuffing poultry.

2 tablespoons oil
1 onion, chopped
2 sticks celery, chopped
2oz (50g/¼ cup) long grain rice
¼ pint (125ml/⅝ cup) stock
2 tablespoons chopped balm leaves
2 tablespoons raisins
salt and pepper

Heat the oil in a small pan. Add the onion and celery and fry for 5 minutes. Stir in the rice and turn in the oil. Add the stock and bring to the boil. Cover and simmer for about 10 minutes or until the rice has absorbed all the stock. Remove from the heat, add the chopped balm and raisins and season to taste. Allow to cool before using.

Balm Stuffing

This delicately flavoured stuffing is very good for fish, chicken, veal or lamb.

2oz (50g/⅔ cup) fresh white or brown breadcrumbs
1oz (25g/2 tablespoons) softened butter or shredded suet
1 tablespoon chopped balm leaves
salt and pepper
1 egg, beaten

Put the breadcrumbs into a basin with the butter or suet, chopped balm and seasoning. Mix well and bind together with the beaten egg.
Variation: Add a crushed clove of garlic.

Hors d'œuvres

Herring Roe Pâté

This is an excellent light pâté for a summer lunch served with Melba toast.

4oz (100g) soft herring roes
salt and pepper
3oz (75g/⅜ cup) butter
1 tablespoon chopped balm leaves

Season the roes with salt and pepper. Melt 1oz (25g/2 tablespoons) of the butter and fry the roes gently for 10 minutes. Pound to a fine paste with a wooden spoon. Soften the remainder of the butter and beat into the roes with the chopped balm. Taste and adjust the seasoning and turn into a serving bowl. Chill lightly before serving. (Serves 4)

Fish

Smoked Haddock Mousse

½ pint (250ml/1¼ cups) water
1 small bay leaf
1 onion, chopped
1lb (400g) smoked haddock
enough aspic-flavoured gelatine to set ½ pint (250ml/1¼ cups)
2 eggs, separated
grated zest and juice ½ lemon
1 tablespoon dry sherry
3 anchovies, finely chopped
1 tablespoon chopped balm leaves
¼ pint (125ml/⅝ cup) double (heavy) cream, lightly whipped
To Garnish:
sliced cucumber

Put the water, bay leaf and onion into a pan, and bring to the boil. Add the haddock and poach gently for 10 minutes or until the fish is cooked. Remove the fish from the pan, take off the skin and bone and flake finely. Strain the liquid and make the aspic up to ½ pint (250ml/1¼ cups) following the instructions on the packet. Allow to cool. Beat the egg yolks with the lemon zest and juice, sherry, anchovies and balm. Beat in the cooled aspic, then stir in the fish. Put on one side and leave until the mixture is beginning to set. Whisk the egg whites until they form soft peaks. Fold first the cream, then the egg whites into the mixture. Turn into a lightly oiled mould or cake tin and refrigerate until set. Turn out shortly before serving and garnish with sliced cucumber. (Serves 6–8)

Meat

Lamb Wrapped in Balm

Although shoulder is the joint given here, other joints, such as leg or loin could be used.

1 large clove garlic
1 shoulder of lamb
salt and pepper
1 bunch of balm (see method)
¼ pint (125ml/⅝ cup) red wine
1 tablespoon chopped balm leaves

Cut the clove of garlic in half and rub it all over the outside of the joint. Season with salt and pepper. Cut enough long, leafy stems of balm to go entirely round the joint and tie them into place with string. Place in a roasting tin (pan) and roast in a moderately hot oven, 375°F, 190°C, Gas Mark 5, allowing 20 minutes to the pound (400g) and 20 minutes over for cooking. Remove the lamb from the tin (pan), place on a heated serving dish and keep warm. Skim off the fat from the meat juices, add the red wine and heat gently. Season to taste and add the chopped balm just before serving with the lamb. (Serves 6)

Poultry

Chicken Breasts with Balm

4 chicken breasts
salt and pepper
2oz (50g/¼ cup) butter
2 tablespoons dry sherry or vermouth
1 tablespoon chopped balm leaves
¼ pint (125ml/⅝ cup) single (light) cream
3oz (75g/¾ cup) Lancashire cheese, grated

Bone out the chicken breasts and season with salt and pepper. Melt the butter and fry the chicken joints for about 12 minutes. Remove from the pan, place on a heated serving dish and keep warm. Add the sherry or vermouth to the pan with the balm and cream and heat gently without boiling. Pour over the chicken and sprinkle with the cheese. Put under a moderate grill (broiler) and grill (broil) until the cheese is golden brown. (Serves 4)

Desserts

Baked Balm Custard

This custard is excellent served well chilled with fresh pineapple and whipped cream.

1 pint (500ml/2½ cups) milk
3 eggs
1½ tablespoons sugar
1 tablespoon chopped balm leaves
pinch grated nutmeg

Heat the milk to blood heat. Beat the eggs and sugar together then add the milk and blend well. Strain into a buttered ovenproof dish. Sprinkle with the balm and nutmeg. Stand in a tin (pan) containing 1 inch (2·5cm) cold water and bake in a slow oven, 300°F, 150°C, Gas Mark 1 for about 1½ hours or until set. Remove from the oven, allow to cool, then chill. (Serves 4)

Balm Stuffed Apples

This gives a delicate flavour to a popular and traditional dessert.

4 medium-sized cooking apples
2 tablespoons ground almonds
1 tablespoon chopped balm leaves
1 tablespoon soft brown sugar
2oz (50g/¼ cup) softened butter

Wash the apples, remove the cores and put into an ovenproof dish. Put the almonds into a basin with the chopped balm, sugar and softened butter and beat until the mixture is well blended. Divide this mixture between the centres of the 4 apples. Cook in a moderate oven, 350°F, 180°C, Gas Mark 4 for 30–40 minutes or until the apples are tender. Serve either hot or cold with cream or ice cream. (Serves 4)

Orange Boodle

2 large oranges
2 tablespoons caster (granulated) sugar
1 tablespoon chopped balm leaves
½ pint (250ml/1¼ cups) soured cream
12 sponge finger biscuits

Grate the zest of 1 orange into a bowl. Cut 4 thin slices of ungrated orange for decoration, then cut each orange in half and squeeze out the juice. Stir the orange zest and juice, sugar and chopped balm into the soured cream. Crumble 1 sponge finger into the bottom of each of 4 glasses and arrange 2 sponge fingers on the inside. Pour in the cream mixture and chill for at least 2 hours. Decorate with halved slices of orange before serving. (Serves 4)

Sweet Yogurt Sauce

This refreshing sauce should be served with fresh fruit, such as apples, strawberries and peaches.

¼ pint (125ml/⅝ cup) natural yogurt
2 tablespoons clear honey
1 tablespoon chopped balm leaves

Put all the ingredients into a bowl. Mix well and leave for at least 15 minutes before serving for the flavours to infuse. (Serves 4)

BASIL

Sweet Basil
(*Ocinum basilicum Labiatae*)
Bush Basil
(*Ocinum minimum*)

A true monarch of herbs, appropriately, since its name is derived from Basileus, the Greek word for King. Once you have cooked with it there is no escape, you become addicted and have to restrain yourself from adding it to every dish.

Sweet basil is a native of south-east Asia, and has been cultivated in Europe for about two thousand years, cosseted as much for its medical and culinary qualities as for its supposed powers in witchcraft, superstitions and religious rites. Bush basil is a miniature variety, no higher than 6–12 inches (15–30cm), more shrubby with a thick mass of small leaves. Sweet basil is more productive, and bush basil more adaptable for growing in pots in the house, on balconies or in window boxes.

A pot of basil in an open window or courtyard, growing or picked, will keep away flies and other disagreeable insects, counteract the effects of foods of suspicious 'freshness', and like so many other herbs, is an aid to digestion.

The whole plant has an exotic, spicy, almost disquieting aroma, released by the lightest touch, which you want to imprison in all manner of ways. The fresh, highly pungent leaves, chopped or shredded, do for tomatoes, turtle soup and liver, what fresh truffles do for egg and meat dishes. Basil transforms simple dishes and adds subtle piquant undertones particularly to tomato and mushroom sauces and soups. It is an essential ingredient of many French, Italian and Greek dishes . . . a tantalising element in stuffings, sausages, omelettes, soufflés, sauces with fish and chicken, and herb butters and in green salads. It is a hardship to leave basil out of anything.

Basil is distinctly a solo turn. Only a cooking spoil-sport would use another fresh herb at the same time in a salad dish. The fresh young leaves should not be cooked but sprinkled at the last moment onto either a cold, or hot dish, so that the rich, warm, slightly peppery clove fragrance flows straight to the taste buds at its fullest. Of the infinite ways in which it casts its spell, I consider it is at its simple best on a tomato salad.

Cultivation
Though basil is a perennial in warm countries, it has to be pampered as a tender annual in temperate climates and rarely stretches to its possible 2–3 feet (65cm–1m). The glossy pale green ovate leaves vary around 2 inches (5cm) long. The flowers are white or purple tinged, insignificant and should not be allowed to develop, or the plants will be more interested in producing seedpods than succulent leaves. Nip out the centres of the young plants as they grow to encourage them into a bushy shape.

Sow basil seed in the open ground after all frosts or cold-snaps are over, in a sheltered sunny place with well-drained fertile soil. Keep them well watered in dry weather. As both types dislike being transplanted . . . root disturbance stunts them . . . it is best to sow a few seeds into individual pots, and when they have germinated, pull out the weaklings and leave the rest to grow on in their pots on a windowsill. In this way you can have basil in the home all through the year.

The first breath of frost kills outdoor basil, but you can rescue as many as you have space for by potting them into richer soil than they enjoyed in the garden, cut them back to the first pair of leaves from the base, and bring them indoors to use as you need.

Preserving

Dried basil is better than no basil at all, though less pungent than fresh. Pick the leaves when they are young and fresh. Discard any brown or discoloured ones. Hang the leaves in bunches in a warm, dry place, away from strong sunlight—an airing cupboard would be ideal. Leave until the leaves are quite dry—the length of time taken to dry them will depend on the temperature and atmosphere of the drying place. When quite dry crumble into airtight jars and label.

Basil freezes well; wash, scissor or chop the leaves and pack tightly into an ice cube tray. Top with water and freeze. When frozen, turn out into polythene bags and store in the freezer. Take out cubes as required, defrost in a strainer, and use as fresh.

Soups

La Soupe au Pistou

This is a Niçoise recipe, rather like Minestrone, into which Pesto is stirred just before serving.

2oz (50g/⅓ cup) haricot (dried white) beans
salt
2 tablespoons olive oil
1 large onion, finely chopped
2 tomatoes, skinned and chopped
2 pints (1 litre/5 cups) stock
4oz (100g) fresh green beans
1 courgette (zucchini), chopped
2 medium-sized potatoes, peeled and diced
1½oz (40g) vermicelli
3 tablespoons pesto sauce (see below)
grated Gruyère (Swiss) cheese for serving
freshly milled black pepper

Soak the haricot (dried white) beans in cold water overnight. Drain, cover with fresh salted water and cook for about 1½ hours until just tender. Drain.
Heat the oil in a large saucepan and fry the onion gently for about 5 minutes. Add the tomatoes and cook for a further 2 minutes. Pour in the stock and bring to the boil. Add the green and haricot (dried white) beans, courgette (zucchini) and potatoes. Cover and simmer gently for 40 minutes, then add the vermicelli and cook for a further 10 minutes. Just before serving, stir in the pesto. Turn into a soup tureen, taste and adjust the seasoning and serve liberally sprinkled with grated cheese. (Serves 4–6)

Sauces

Fresh Tomato Sauce

This sauce is traditionally served with spaghetti and other pasta but it is also excellent with chicken, veal escalopes, or meat loaves.

2 tablespoons olive oil
2 cloves garlic, crushed
6 large tomatoes, skinned and chopped
6–8 anchovy fillets, chopped (optional)
1 tablespoon chopped basil
salt and pepper

Heat the oil in a pan and fry the garlic for 2 minutes. Add the tomatoes and chopped anchovies if using. Cover and cook gently for 10 minutes. Add the basil and seasoning (if anchovies have been used, you will probably not need any salt) and heat gently for 2 minutes. (Serves 4)

Pesto

This is a famous Genoese sauce generally served with spaghetti or gnocchi, but it is also added to Soupe au Pistou (see above). If you want to you can make up a larger quantity and store it in a jar covered with olive oil.

2oz (50g) basil leaves
1–2 cloves garlic
pinch salt
1oz (25g/¼ cup) pine nuts or chopped walnuts
3 tablespoons grated Parmesan or Sardo cheese
4 tablespoons olive oil

Remove the stalks from the basil and pound the

leaves in a mortar with the garlic, salt and nuts. When it is smooth, add the cheese and mix well. G adually add the olive oil, stirring steadily so that the oil becomes properly amalgamated; at the end the sauce should resemble creamed butter. (Serves 4)

Fish

Baked Red Mullet with Basil

4 red mullet
¼ pint (125ml/⅝ cup) olive oil
4 tablespoons lemon juice
2 cloves garlic, crushed
salt and freshly milled black pepper
1 lemon, sliced
1 tablespoon chopped basil

Take four pieces of foil large enough to cover the fish. Brush with oil and place the cleaned mullet in the centre. Mix the oil and lemon juice together and add the garlic and seasoning. Spoon over the fish. Arrange a couple of lemon slices on top. Bring up the sides of the foil and fold over so that the fish is completely encased and place on a baking sheet. Bake in a moderate oven, 350°F, 180°C, Gas Mark 4 for 30 minutes. Open out the foil and sprinkle with the basil before serving. (Serves 4)

Meat

Lamb's Liver with Basil

8oz (200g) bacon rashers (slices)
2 tablespoons flour
salt and pepper
1lb (400g) lamb's liver, sliced
1oz (25g/2 tablespoons) lard or dripping (see method)
generous ¼ pint (150ml/1 cup) stock or wine
2 tablespoons chopped basil

Fry the bacon rashers (slices) in a pan without any fat. Remove from the pan, place on a heated serving dish and keep warm. Season the flour with salt and pepper and toss the slices of liver in this. Heat the fat in the frying pan (if the bacon was fairly fatty it may not be necessary to add any extra fat) and fry the slices of liver for about 8 minutes. Remove from the pan and place on the dish with the bacon. Add the stock or wine to the juices remaining in the pan and bring to the boil. Add the basil, taste and adjust the seasoning and pour over the liver. (Serves 4)

Arancini Siciliani
(Savoury Rice Balls)

These Sicilian oranges are made of rice with a savoury filling and the basil is used to make the leaves of the oranges.

8oz (200g/1⅓ cups) long grain rice
1 pint (500ml/2½ cups) water
salt
2oz (50g/½ cup) grated Parmesan cheese
1 large egg, beaten
½ pint (250ml/1¼ cups) Tomato Sauce (see above)
freshly milled black pepper
2oz (50g) Bel Paese cheese
2oz (50g) cooked ham or salami
2oz (50g/⅔ cup) fresh white breadcrumbs
oil for deep frying
about 24 basil leaves

Put the rice into a pan with the water and ½ teaspoon salt. Cover, bring to the boil and simmer gently for 15 minutes or until the rice is tender and has absorbed all the liquid. Turn the rice into a bowl, stir in the Parmesan cheese and the egg and 1 tablespoon of the tomato sauce. Season with salt and pepper and leave until the rice is quite cold. Dice the Bel Paese cheese and chop the ham or salami finely. Put into a bowl and stir in 2 tablespoons of the tomato sauce. Season with salt and pepper. Flour your hands well to prevent the rice from sticking, then take just under a tablespoonful of rice and mould it into a ball. Make a hollow in the centre and spoon in a teaspoonful of the ham stuffing. Put a little more rice on top and shape into a ball. This quantity of mixture will make about 12 balls, about 1½ inches (3·75 cm) in diameter. Coat the balls thickly in the breadcrumbs. Heat the oil to 350°F, 180°C, then fry the balls a few at a time until crisp and golden brown. Drain well and garnish with the basil leaves just before serving. Heat the remainder of the tomato sauce and serve with the oranges. (Serves 4—6)

Vegetables and Salads

Baked Tomatoes and Basil

1lb (400g) tomatoes, sliced
salt and pepper
1 tablespoon chopped basil
2 onions, sliced
2oz (50g/⅔ cup) fresh white or brown
 breadcrumbs
1oz (25g/2 tablespoons) butter

Put a layer of tomatoes into the bottom of a well buttered ovenproof dish. Season with salt and pepper, sprinkle with some of the basil and top with a layer of onions. Repeat these layers until all the tomatoes and onions have been used up. Sprinkle thickly with the breadcrumbs and dot with the butter. Bake in a moderate oven, 350°F, 180°C, Gas Mark 4 for 50 minutes or until golden brown. (Serves 4)

Variation: Sprinkle the tomatoes with a pinch of sugar as well as the seasoning and basil.

Insalata di Fagioli

(Italian Bean Salad)

12oz (300g/2 cups) shelled fresh broad,
 lima or haricot beans
salt
1 large clove garlic
4oz (100g) lean ham, finely chopped
3 tablespoons olive oil
1½ tablespoons lemon juice or wine vinegar
freshly milled black pepper
2 teaspoons chopped basil

Cook the beans in boiling salted water until just tender, but still crisp. Drain well. Cut the clove of garlic in half and rub it all over the inside of a salad bowl. Add the beans and ham. Beat the oil with the lemon juice or vinegar and seasoning. Pour over the beans and mix well. Allow to cool and chill. Sprinkle with the basil just before serving. (Serves 4)

Tomato Salad

This is one of the simplest, but most delicious of all basil recipes.

1 clove garlic
6 large tomatoes
3 tablespoons olive oil
1 tablespoon wine vinegar
salt and freshly milled black pepper
1 tablespoon chopped basil

Cut the clove of garlic in half and rub all round the inside of the salad bowl or dish. Slice the tomatoes and place in the dish. Blend the oil with the vinegar and seasoning. Pour over the tomatoes and sprinkle with the basil just before serving. (Serves 4)

Raw Spinach Salad

4 tablespoons olive oil
2 tablespoons wine vinegar
1½ tablespoons chopped basil
finely grated zest 1 lemon
salt and pepper
4oz (100g) spinach leaves
1 small lettuce heart
8 radishes, sliced
6 spring onions (scallions), chopped

Put the oil, vinegar, basil, lemon zest and seasoning into a screw-topped jar and shake well. Discard any tough stems from the spinach and wash and dry well. Wash and dry the lettuce. Tear the spinach and lettuce into small pieces and put into a salad bowl with the radishes and spring onions (scallions). Just before serving add the dressing and toss well. (Serves 4)

Desserts

Soufflé Omelette with Basil

2 teaspoons chopped basil
1 tablespoon caster sugar
2 eggs, separated
½ oz (15g/1 tablespoon) butter
1 tablespoon lemon juice

Pound the basil with half the sugar into a fine, pale green, aromatic paste. Beat the egg yolks lightly with the remaining sugar. Whisk the egg whites until they form stiff peaks, then fold into the yolks. Heat the butter in an omelette pan until it is bubbling. Add the egg mixture and spread it evenly over the pan. Allow to cook for about 4 minutes, then place the frying pan under a moderate grill for about 6 minutes until the omelette is a very pale golden. Slide on to a heated serving plate and sprinkle with the basil mixture and lemon juice. (Serves 1–2)

24

BAY

(Laurus nobilis)

The sweet bay is the original laurel the Romans and Greeks fashioned into wreaths with which to crown their heroes and poets ... hence 'Poet Laureate'. It should not be confused with the poisonous cherry laurel (Prunus laurocerasus), often used as hedging or in shrubberies. There is little risk of a mistake once a leaf is picked and torn ... the sweet bay is intensely pungent and aromatic; the cherry laurel is not.

An evergreen bush or tree, bay is a native of the Mediterranean area, though surprisingly hardy in colder climates where it reaches 10–12 feet (3–4 metres). Even large trees and hedges, killed to ground level in an occasional exceptionally severe winter, surprisingly recover and shoot up again from the base, reaching their former dignity in two or three years.

Bay leaves have an affinity with a remarkable variety of differing foods; they seem to want to get invited into everything. Apart from being an essential member of a bouquet garni, the others being thyme, marjoram and parsley, they are also used in soups, casseroles, under and over roast meat, in white or tomato sauces, cooked with salted or pickled tongue, pork and other meats and stuffings for fish and poultry. Cook them with almost any vegetable, particularly Jerusalem artichokes to add a subtle difference. They can also be added to sweet custards and rice puddings or other milk dishes which need long and slow cooking. Bay leaves can be used dried or fresh. Always break the edges of fresh bay leaves to release the pungent oils before using them in cooking. Be cautious too, never heavy handed; one or at the most two leaves, are usually enough to flavour any dish, savoury or sweet, for four people. Remove the leaves if possible before serving ... they are not intended for eating.

Cultivation

In warm climates, left unrestrained, the bay becomes a densely foliaged tree about 40 feet (12 metres) high, of a pyramid shape. For less ambitious growers it is easily tamed into a domestic 'pet'; in tubs at the front doors of town houses; carved into various shapes on patios, and even kept 'dwarfed' and potted in the kitchen for instant use. When grown in tubs for formal and ornamental use, the bay is generally trained as a standard on a single stem, cutting off side shoots as they form to encourage the top growth. This can be any shape you fancy, ball, square, helmet ... and trimmed a few times during the summer. This should be done with secateurs not shears, to avoid the distressing sight of sliced maltreated leaves. For this reason it is wise to keep the shape simple and not indulge in fanciful topiary work. Save the trimmings to dry or use fresh.

For a permanent place in the garden, plant bay in well-drained soil where it is sheltered from strong north and east winds.

It propagates readily from cuttings of half-ripe shoots about 4 inches (10cm) long, taken in late summer and potted into rooting compost. Infant mortality, alas, is high, so take more cuttings than you can possibly wish to grow, and put the pots outside in a variety of sheltered places . . . full sun, semi-shade, complete shade. Bring them inside if severe frost is threatened, and plant them in their permanent homes, in tubs or the open garden, the following autumn.

A haphazard (hit or miss) method of propagation, often more successful than careful nursing, is simply to stick the cuttings in open ground in various parts of the garden in groups, and replant any which survive, the following autumn. In winter it is also advisable to pack sacking round the roots of young plants to protect them from frost.

Preserving

Bay leaves can be used fresh or dry and are very simple to dry. Pick them individually or cut off sprays with secateurs. Leave in a cool, airy, shaded place for a few days then pack into airtight jars.

Bouquet Garni

The constituents of a bouquet garni, used in so many long cooking dishes and for marinades, varies according to the dish in which it is being used, but the bay leaf should always be there. The most common form is a bay leaf with a sprig of thyme, marjoram and parsley all tied together with a piece of fine string. In Provençal cooking for meat casseroles a piece of peeled orange zest is often added as well.

Soups

Potage Parmentier

2oz (50g/¼ cup) butter
1½lb (600g) potatoes, peeled and sliced
2 large onions, chopped
¾ pint (375ml/2 cups) stock
¾ pint (375ml/2 cups) milk
salt and pepper
1 bay leaf
1 egg yolk
4 tablespoons double (heavy) cream
2 tablespoons chopped parsley

Melt the butter in a large pan and gently fry the potatoes and onions for about 10 minutes. Pour in the stock and milk and add the seasoning and bay leaf. Cover the pan and simmer gently for 20 minutes. Either put the vegetables into a liquidizer and blend for a minute or put the vegetables through a sieve or vegetable mouli, then blend with the strained stock. Turn the soup back into the saucepan and bring to the boil. Blend the egg yolk with the cream, then stir in about 4 tablespoons of the hot soup. Pour this back into the pan and heat gently, but do not allow the soup to boil.

Turn into a soup tureen and sprinkle with parsley before serving. (Serves 4-6)

Tourin de Catalonia
(Spanish Onion Soup)

2 tablespoons oil
2 large onions, finely sliced
2oz (50g) ham, chopped
1 stick celery, chopped
1 sprig thyme
pinch grated nutmeg
1 bay leaf
salt and pepper
¼ pint (125ml/⅝ cup) white wine
3 pints (1·5 litres/7½ cups) stock
2 egg yolks
1 teaspoon vinegar

Heat the oil in a large pan. Add the onions, ham, celery, thyme, nutmeg, bay leaf and seasoning and cook over a very gentle heat for 10 minutes, without allowing the onions to brown. Add the wine and stock and simmer for 15 minutes. Remove the bay leaf and thyme. Beat the egg yolks in a soup tureen and add the vinegar. Pour in the hot soup and mix well. Serve with fried bread croûtons. (Serves 4–6)

Sauces

Béchamel Sauce

This is one of the classic sauces which is used as a base for any number of dishes, but would not be the same without its bay leaf.

generous ½ pint (300ml/1½ cups) milk
1 bay leaf
3 peppercorns
1 blade mace

few parsley stalks
a piece of carrot
½ small onion, chopped
1oz (25g/2 tablespoons) butter
1oz (25g/4 tablespoons) flour
salt and pepper

Put the milk into a saucepan with the bay leaf, peppercorns, mace, parsley, carrot and onion. Bring slowly to the boil, cover and simmer very gently for 10 minutes, then strain. Melt the butter in a clean saucepan, add the flour and cook gently for about 2 minutes. Remove the pan from the heat and very gradually beat in the strained milk. Return the pan to the heat and bring to the boil, stirring all the time until the sauce is smooth and thick.
Makes ½ pint (250ml/1¼ cups)

Fish

Soused Herrings

These herrings can either be served hot or are delicious served cold with soured cream.

6 herrings
salt and pepper
¼ pint (125ml/⅝ cup) vinegar
¼ pint (125ml/⅝ cup) water
1 tablespoon mixed pickling spice
4 bay leaves
2 small onions, sliced

Scale, clean and bone the herrings. Season well with salt and pepper. Roll up the fillets, skin outwards, from the tail end. Place neatly in an ovenproof dish. Cover with the vinegar and water and sprinkle with the pickling spice, bay leaves and onions. Cover and cook in a slow oven, 300°F, 150°C, Gas Mark 2 for 1½ hours. (Serves 6)

Meat

Irish Spiced Brisket of Beef

4lb (1·75 kilo) boned brisket of beef
10oz (250g/¾ cup) coarse salt
2 shallots, finely chopped
3 bay leaves
1 teaspoon saltpetre
1 teaspoon allspice
6 tablespoons brown sugar
1 teaspoon ground cloves
1 teaspoon ground mace

6 peppercorns, lightly crushed
1 tablespoon chopped thyme
1 onion, chopped
2 carrots, peeled and chopped

Put the meat into a large bowl. Rub it on all sides with 8 oz (200g/½ cup) of the salt. Cover and leave for 24 hours in a refrigerator or cool place. Add the remaining salt to the bowl with the shallots, bay leaves, saltpetre, allspice, brown sugar, cloves, mace, peppercorns and thyme. Rub this well into the beef and leave for 7 days, turning the beef and rubbing well with the spice mixture every day. Pour off any liquid which forms. Remove the meat from the bowl, roll up and tie securely with string. Put the meat into a large saucepan with the onion and carrots, cover with cold water and bring to the boil. Remove any scum, then cover and simmer very gently for 4–5 hours or until the meat is very tender. Allow to cool in the cooking liquor, then lift it out. Place it between two boards with a heavy weight on top and leave to press for 8 hours. (Serves 8–10)

Vegetables and Salads

Lentil Salad

For this salad it is essential to use green or brown lentils, not the orange ones which break up and become mushy.

8oz (200g/1 cup) green or brown lentils
1 bay leaf
2 onions
salt and pepper
4 tablespoons oil
2 tablespoons vinegar
¼ teaspoon dry mustard
1 tablespoon chopped parsley

Put the lentils into a saucepan with the bay leaf, one of the onions, roughly chopped, and seasoning. Cover with cold water. Bring to the boil, cover and simmer gently for about 1 hour or until the lentils are just tender, but not mushy. Drain. Finely chop the remaining onion and add to the hot lentils with the oil, vinegar, mustard, parsley and extra seasoning. Mix well and leave until cold. (Serves 4)

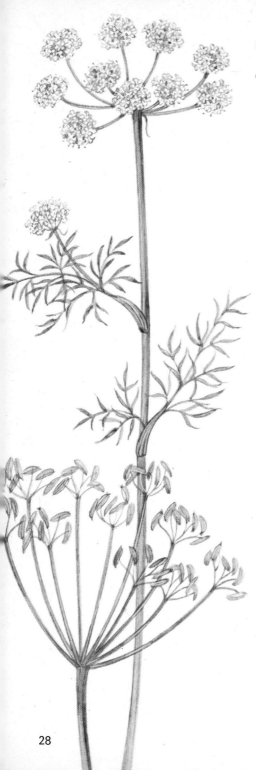

CARAWAY

(*Carum carvi*)

Not an essential herb, whose absence, you feel would wreck (distract from) your cooking, but worth growing for the unexpectedness of its flavour in certain dishes.

It is one of the many delicate-looking umbellifers which are not easy to distinguish between until they flower and seed. A native of Europe it grows widely and easily. A biennial plant, it has ribbed stems and grows 2–3 feet (65cm–1 metre) with finely divided leaves similar to those of a carrot. The modest white flattened flower heads about 2 inches (5cm) across begin to form in early summer and are far from spectacular. It is, however, the sickle-shaped, ribbed aromatic seeds which follow that makes them such a popular commercial crop.

The young green needle-fine leaves, though lacking the immediate pungency of the mature seeds, add a delicate difference finely chopped in salads, or scattered onto soup at the last moment. The thick tapered roots too may be used as a vegetable, boiled and eaten like carrots.

As for the precious and all important seeds, these got off to a bad start with me, having been impelled to eat 'seed cake' as a child. It was only many years later when I met the unmistakable flavour unexpectedly in savoury dishes that we became not just 'good friends' but allies. They do mysterious things for cabbage, onions, potatoes and vegetable dishes, tripe, pork, liver, certain cheeses, meat and fish dishes, as well as carrying out their known flavouring functions in bread, pickles, cakes and sauerkraut.

One of the gentler rather than aromatic uses of caraway seed is to help digestion . . . they were always added to any dish likely to cause flatulence, including baked apples, and cabbage. Caraway has been used for centuries because of the digestive properties of the seeds, leaves and roots, to help glands, kidneys and generally give you an entire 'spring clean'. On a more elevated level caraway seed oil is used in many liqueurs, notably Kümmel . . . the German name for caraway, and it was put into love potions because it was believed to stop the pair from straying!

Cultivation
Sow the seed in late spring in a sunny well-drained border, and thin the seedlings to about 9 inches (22·5cm) apart, or as soon as they are big enough to handle; the roots are too fragile to transplant. Water the young plants in very dry weather. The seeds will ripen in late summer the following year.

Preserving
As soon as the flower umbels go brown, cut the plants down to ground level and hang the stems upside down in small bunches over a container lined with cloth or paper, in an airy shed, or similar place, until the seeds are fully ripe and willing to be shaken out. Store in airtight jars.

Soups

Scandinavian Caraway Leaf Soup

This soup can be served on its own, but is more commonly served in individual bowls with a poached egg floating on the top.

1oz (25g/2 tablespoons) butter
1oz (25g/4 tablespoons) flour
2 pints (1 litre/5 cups) veal or chicken stock
4 tablespoons chopped caraway leaves
1 egg yolk
2 tablespoons double (heavy) or single (light) cream
salt and pepper

Melt the butter in a pan, add the flour and cook for a minute. Gradually stir in the stock and bring to the boil, stirring all the time. Add 3 tablespoons of the caraway leaves and simmer gently for 10 minutes. Beat the egg yolk and cream in a basin. Add a little of the hot soup and blend well, then pour back into the hot soup and stir well. Do not allow the soup to boil after the egg and cream have been added. Taste and adjust the seasoning before serving, sprinkled with the remaining chopped caraway leaves. (Serves 4–6)
Note: For a simple caraway seed soup, simmer 1 teaspoon caraway seeds in the stock for 30 minutes. Strain, then continue as above omitting the caraway leaves.

Meat

Austrian Roast Beef

2lb (800g) boned and rolled rib of beef
2 large onions, finely chopped
2 tablespoons caraway seeds
salt
1oz (25g/2 tablespoons) bacon fat or dripping
2 tablespoons vinegar
freshly milled black pepper
2lb (800g) beef bones
2 tablespoons flour

Unroll the beef and lay it out flat on a board. Mix 2 tablespoons of the onion with 1 tablespoon of the caraway seeds and a good pinch of salt. Spread the meat with this mixture, reroll and tie securely with string. Put the bacon fat or dripping into a roasting tin (pan) with the remaining onion. Put into a moderately hot oven, 375°F, 190°C, Gas Mark 5 for 5 minutes. Put the meat in the centre of the tin (pan) and sprinkle with the remaining caraway seeds, vinegar and seasoning. Arrange the beef bones round the joint and pour in enough water to come a quarter of the way up the meat. Roast for 1 hour, basting from time to time. Remove the meat from the pan, place on a heated serving dish and keep warm. Remove and discard the beef bones. Skim off 2 tablespoons of the fat from the top of the juices in the tin (pan). Put into a saucepan and stir in the flour. Cook over a low heat until the flour is a rich golden brown. Gradually stir in the liquid from the meat together with the onion and bring to the boil, stirring all the time. Taste and adjust the seasoning and serve this sauce with the beef. (Serves 4-6)

Sauerkraut mit Knackwurst

15oz (425g) can or jar sauerkraut
1 large cooking apple, peeled, cored and
  grated
2 carrots, peeled and grated
2oz (50g/¼ cup) butter, melted
1 teaspoon caraway seeds
freshly milled black pepper
4 thick slices streaky (fat) or flank bacon
4 knackwurst or 8 frankfurter sausages

Soak the sauerkraut for 15 minutes in cold water then wring dry in your hands. Put the apple, carrots, butter, sauerkraut, caraway seeds and pepper into a bowl and mix well. Turn this into a casserole and top with the bacon. Cover and cook in a moderately hot oven, 375°F, 190°C, Gas Mark 5 for 45 minutes. Arrange the sausages on top and bake uncovered for a further 15 minutes. (Serves 4)

Hungarian Goulash

1½lb (600g) good quality stewing beef
1oz (25g/4 tablespoons) flour
1 teaspoon salt
1½ tablespoons paprika
1oz (25g/2 tablespoons) dripping
1 large onion, chopped
1lb (400g) tomatoes, skinned and quartered
¾ pint (375ml/2 cups) beef stock
1 teaspoon caraway seeds
1lb (400g) potatoes, peeled and sliced
¼ pint (125ml/⅝ cup) soured cream

Cut the beef into 1½ inch (3·75cm) cubes and toss in the flour, seasoned with salt and paprika. Melt the dripping in a pan, add the onion and fry for a few minutes. Add the meat and cook for a further 5 minutes, stirring until the meat is evenly browned. Add the tomatoes and gradually stir in the stock. Bring to the boil, stirring all the time. Add the caraway seeds and the potatoes, cover the pan and simmer gently for 2½ hours. Remove from the heat, allow to cool for a minute, then stir in the soured cream. Taste and adjust the seasoning. (Serves 4)

Caraway Dumplings

These dumplings are generally served with Veal Paprika or Goulash in Hungary, but can be served with any meat casserole or thick soup.

4oz (100g/1 cup) plain (all-purpose) flour
1 teaspoon baking powder
½ teaspoon salt
¼ teaspoon caraway seeds
freshly milled black pepper
1½oz (40g/3 tablespoons) butter or lard
cold water

Sift together the flour, baking powder and salt. Add the caraway seeds and pepper. Rub in the butter or lard until the mixture resembles fine breadcrumbs and bind with water to give a soft, but not sticky dough. Roll into balls, about the size of a walnut and cook in boiling water for 20–30 minutes or until light and fluffy. (Serves 4)

Vegetables and Salads

Paprika Cabbage

1 small white cabbage
3 tablespoons vinegar
1 teaspoon caraway seeds
salt and freshly milled black pepper
3oz (75g/⅜ cup) butter
1 large onion, sliced
1 teaspoon paprika
1 green pepper (capsicum), de-seeded and
  finely sliced

Shred the cabbage finely and put into a bowl with the vinegar, caraway seeds and seasoning. Leave to marinate for 12 hours, turning from time to time. Melt the butter in a pan and fry the onion for 5 minutes, add the cabbage and sprinkle over the paprika. Cover and simmer gently for 1 hour. Just before serving, stir in the pepper (capsicum), and taste and adjust the seasoning. (Serves 4–6)

Beans in Soured Cream

1lb (400g) runner beans
salt
¼ pint (125ml/⅝ cup) soured cream
¼ teaspoon grated nutmeg
½ teaspoon caraway seeds
freshly milled black pepper
2oz (50g/¼ cup) butter
2oz (50g/⅔ cup) fresh, white breadcrumbs

Top, tail, string and slice the beans. Cook in boiling salted water for 5 minutes, then drain well. Mix the soured cream with the nutmeg, caraway seeds and seasoning. Add the beans and toss well together. Well grease an oven-proof dish with some of the butter. Melt the remaining butter and toss the breadcrumbs in this. Turn the beans into the dish, cover with the breadcrumbs and bake in a moderate oven, 350°F, 180°C, Gas Mark 4 for 20–30 minutes or until topping is crisp and golden. (Serves 4)

Turkish Fried Carrots

If preferred the caraway here can be replaced with a tablespoon of chopped mint.

1lb (400g) carrots
salt
1 tablespoon flour
freshly milled black pepper
3 tablespoons olive oil
¼ pint (250ml/1¼ cups) natural yogurt
1 teaspoon caraway seeds

Peel the carrots and cut into slices. Cook in boiling salted water for 10 minutes, then drain thoroughly. Season the flour with salt and pepper and toss the carrots in this. Heat the oil in a frying pan and fry the carrots on both sides until golden brown. Place in a heated serving dish and keep warm. Heat the yogurt in a small pan, but do not allow it to boil. Pour over the carrots and sprinkle with the caraway just before serving. (Serves 4)

Cakes and Breads

Yorkshire Gingerbread

8oz (200g/1 cup) butter
¾ pint (375ml/2 cups) black treacle
8oz (200g/2 cups) sultanas (golden raisins)
8oz (200g/2 cups) chopped candied peel
8oz (200g/1⅓ cups) soft brown sugar
1 tablespoon bicarbonate of soda
1 tablespoon ground coriander
1 tablespoon ground cloves
2 teaspoons caraway seeds
2 tablespoons ground ginger
2 eggs, beaten
1¼lb (500g/5 cups) plain (all-purpose) flour

Grease and line a 10 inch (25cm) square cake tin. Put the butter and treacle into a saucepan over a moderate heat. Leave until the butter has melted then remove from the heat. Put the sultanas (golden raisins), peel, sugar, soda,

coriander, cloves, caraway seeds and ginger into a large mixing bowl. Pour in the butter and treacle and mix well and beat in the eggs. Gradually sift in the flour and beat well to blend. Spoon into the tin and smooth the top. Bake in a slow oven, 300°F, 150°C, Gas Mark 1 for 3 hours. Turn out of the tin and cool on a wire rack. Store in a cake tin for 1 week before using.

Pretzels

1 teaspoon sugar
generous ¼ pint (150ml/1 cup) warm milk
2 teaspoons dried yeast
12oz (300g/3 cups) plain (all-purpose) flour
½ teaspoon fine salt
1oz (25g/2 tablespoons) butter
1 tablespoon caraway seeds
1 egg, lightly beaten
2 teaspoons coarse salt

Dissolve the sugar in the milk. Sprinkle over the yeast and leave in a warm place for 10 minutes or until frothy. Sift the flour with the fine salt. Rub in the butter, then add 2 teaspoons of the caraway seeds. Make a well in the centre of the flour and pour in the yeast liquid. Draw the flour into the liquid and continue mixing until the dough comes away from the sides of the bowl; add extra warm milk, if necessary. Turn out on to a floured surface and knead for about 10 minutes or until the dough feels smooth and elastic. Put into an oiled polythene bag and put into a warm place for about 45 minutes or until the dough has doubled in size.
Place the dough on a floured working surface, and form into a 12 inch (30cm) roll. Cut into 48 pieces with a knife. Roll the pieces between your hands to make 6 inch (15cm) long sausages. Place on the working surface and curve the ends towards yourself. Cross the loop half way along each side and twist once. Bend the ends back and press firmly on to the curve of the loop.
Half fill a large pan with water. Bring to the boil and drop the pretzels in a few at a time. Cook for 1 minute or until they rise to the surface. Remove from the pan with a slotted spoon, drain thoroughly, then place on greased baking sheets. Brush with beaten egg and sprinkle with the remaining caraway seeds and the coarse salt. Bake in a moderately hot oven, 375°F, 190°C, Gas Mark 5 for 15 minutes or until golden brown. Cool on a wire rack. (Makes 48)

CHERVIL

(Anthriscus cerefolium)

One of the unforgettable spring scents and tastes, which cannot truly be replaced till the next spring. Nothing throughout the rest of the year quite captures the first breath of the warm, spicy, slightly aniseed flavour, heralding spring as evocatively as the primrose, dawn chorus, the first cuckoo, or asparagus . . . depending on where you live.

It is a quick-growing hardy annual, with feathery light green leaves which resemble parsley, and can replace it when there is a lapse in the parsley crop, as it is much easier to grow. The plants are insignificant and reach $1-1\frac{1}{2}$ feet (30–50cm), so can easily be used as path edging or in patches in a flower border between dominant eye-catchers.

The warm, spicy, slightly aniseed flavour and aroma of chervil is unhappily quite lost in long cooking. The fresh chopped leaves must be sprinkled on at the last moment to make their unusual impact to egg dishes, sauces, salads, soups and particularly to new buttered potatoes, young carrots and baby broad beans. Even as a garnish for hors d'oeuvres the leaves should be chopped and added only minutes before the food is to be eaten, since the evanescent flavour wilts rapidly. A sprinkling of chervil will turn any nondescript iced soup into something quite unordinary,

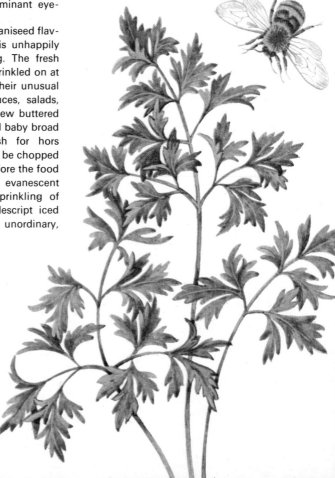

and to be remembered. Worked densely into butter and chilled, chervil makes a welcome difference to grilled (broiled) steak or sole.

Cultivation

The seeds germinate quickly (unlike parsley) and can be sown throughout the spring and summer at regular intervals so there is always a supply, though none will taste like the fresh spring ones. Sow where they are to grow, preferably in semi-shade as they quickly run to seed. When the leaves lose their fresh green and threaten to go brown, this is not a dreaded threat of rust disease, but a call for help . . . they cannot go on much longer and want you to sow more seed. If a few heads are left on when the leaves are being gathered they will conveniently re-seed themselves, as it stays viable for only a short time. However you must be sure the position can be permanent for the seedlings cannot be transplanted. Alternatively cut down the flower stems, or better still pinch out the flowers at bud stage to stop the plants running to seed. Always pick the leaves from the outside of the cluster as you do parsley, to keep the centre producing new ones.

Chervil is a most agreeable and well-behaved herb to grow in pots or boxes in the house to keep up a winter supply; one kept on a kitchen window sill will ensure that it is used as constantly as it is entitled to be.

Preserving

Chervil can be dried but it is better to freeze it if this is possible. To dry the leaves pick them when they are young and fresh. Discard any brown or discoloured ones. Hang the leaves in bunches in a warm dry place, the airing cupboard would be ideal, away from strong sunlight. Leave until the leaves are quite dry—the length of time taken to dry them will depend on the temperature and atmosphere of the drying place. When quite dry crumble into airtight jars and label.

To freeze, wash, scissor or chop the leaves and pack tightly into an ice cube tray. Top with water and freeze. When frozen, turn out into plastic bags and store in the freezer. Take out cubes as required, defrost in a strainer, and use as fresh. Alternatively, pack small bunches into polythene bags and freeze. If you want to store the chervil for more than 2 months, blanch first in boiling water, drain, dip in cold water then dry well, pack and freeze.

Hors d'œuvres

Chervil and Avocado Mousse

2 avocado pears
2 tablespoons lemon juice
4 tablespoons double (heavy) cream
salt and freshly milled black pepper
1 clove garlic, crushed (optional)
2 tablespoons chopped chervil

Cut the pears in half, remove the stones, then carefully scoop out the flesh, being careful not to damage the skins. Mash the flesh or put into a blender, and add the lemon juice, cream, seasoning, and garlic, if wished. Pile back into the avocado skins and sprinkle with the chervil. Cover tightly with foil, to trap the chervil flavour, and chill until ready to serve. Serve with fingers of crisp dry toast. (Serves 4)

Soups

Chervil Soup

1oz (25g/2 tablespoons) butter
1oz (25g/4 tablespoons) flour
1 pint (500ml/2½ cups) light stock
4 tablespoons chopped chervil
salt and pepper
1 tablespoon fresh or soured cream

Melt the butter in a pan, add the flour and cook for a minute. Gradually stir in the stock and bring to the boil, stirring all the time. Add 3 tablespoons of the chervil, cover and simmer gently for 20 minutes. Taste and adjust the seasoning, stir in the cream and serve the soup sprinkled with the remaining chopped chervil. (Serves 2—3)

Chervil and Potato Soup

This can either make a warming lunch on its own, or be served in smaller quantities at the start of a meal.

1oz (25g/2 tablespoons) butter
1lb (400g) potatoes, peeled and sliced
4 leeks or onions, chopped
1½ pints (750ml/3¾ cups) stock
1 blade mace
1 bay leaf
¼ pint (125ml/⅝ cup) single (light) cream or milk
salt and pepper
6 tablespoons chopped chervil

Melt the butter in a pan, add the potatoes and leeks or onions, cover and cook gently for 10 minutes. Add the stock, mace and bay leaf, cover and simmer for 40 minutes. Remove the bay leaf and mace and either put the soup into a liquidizer and blend for a minute, or put the vegetables through a sieve or vegetable mouli, then blend with the strained stock. Return to the pan, stir in the cream or milk and season to taste. Reheat gently without boiling, then remove from the heat and stir in the chervil. Serve at once with fried croûtons, if wished. (Serves 4–6)

Fish

Chervil Sauce with Scallops

1lb (400g) scallops
2oz (50g/¼ cup) butter
1oz (25g/4 tablespoons) flour
½ pint (250ml/1¼ cups) milk or veal or chicken stock
2 teaspoons finely chopped or grated onion
2 heaped tablespoons chopped chervil
4oz (100g/1 cup) grated Gruyère (Swiss) cheese
3 tablespoons dry breadcrumbs (raspings)
salt and pepper

Clean the scallops, remove the outer membrane, leave the corals separate (they barely need cooking) and cut the white parts in half or quarters if large. Melt half the butter in a pan, add the scallops and cook for a few minutes, turning them all the time. Put in the corals for the last 30 seconds cooking. Remove the scallops with a slotted spoon and put on one side. Melt the remaining butter in the pan. Stir in the flour and cook for a minute, then gradually stir in the milk or stock and bring to the boil, stirring all the time. Add the onion, scallops and chervil and season to taste. Spoon into 6 small or 4 larger, ovenproof dishes. Mix the cheese with the breadcrumbs and sprinkle over the top. Bake in a hot oven, 425°F, 220°C, Gas Mark 7 for 10 minutes or until the top is golden brown. (Serves 4–6)

Eggs

Chervil Soufflé

1oz (25g/2 tablespoons) butter
1oz (25g/4 tablespoons) flour
generous ¼ pint (150ml/1 cup) milk
3oz (75g/¾ cup) Cheddar cheese, grated
4 eggs, separated
salt and freshly milled black pepper
1 tablespoon chopped chervil

Melt the butter in a large pan, add the flour and cook for a minute. Remove from the heat and gradually stir in the milk then return to the heat and bring to the boil, stirring all the time until the sauce thickens. Remove from the heat and beat in the cheese, the egg yolks, one at a time, then the seasoning and chervil. Whisk the egg whites until they form stiff peaks, then fold into the cheese mixture. Turn into a 2½ pint (1·25 litre, 6¼ cup) soufflé dish and bake in a moderately hot oven, 375°F, 190°C, Gas Mark 5 for 30 minutes or until well risen and golden brown. (Serves 3–4)

Eggs with Chervil

4 eggs
2oz (50g/¼ cup) butter
2 teaspoons lemon juice
2 tablespoons chopped chervil

Put the eggs into boiling water and cook for exactly 5 minutes. Remove the pan from the heat and place under running cold water. As soon as the eggs are cool enough to handle, lightly tap the shells all over with the back of a spoon. Replace the eggs in the pan and leave under cold running water for a further 2–3 minutes until they are quite cold, then very carefully remove the shells.
Melt the butter in a large shallow pan. Add the eggs and lemon juice and cook, stirring all the time for about 5 minutes. Sprinkle with the chervil just before serving. (Serves 2 or 4)

Variation: Replace the butter with $\frac{1}{4}$ pint (125ml/$\frac{5}{8}$ cup) single (light) cream and omit the lemon juice.

Vegetables and Salads

Buttered Peas

Chervil enhances the flavour of fresh peas and is also excellent for adding flavour to frozen peas.

2oz (50g/$\frac{1}{4}$ cup) butter
1 bunch spring onions (scallions), chopped
1lb (400g/2$\frac{2}{3}$ cups) fresh shelled peas
$\frac{1}{4}$ pint (125ml/$\frac{5}{8}$ cup) chicken stock
salt and freshly milled black pepper
1 tablespoon chopped chervil

Melt the butter in a pan, add the spring onions (scallions) and cook gently for 2 minutes. Add the peas, stock and seasoning, cover and simmer gently for 10 minutes. Remove the lid and simmer for a further 5–10 minutes to evaporate some of the liquid and until the peas are tender. Turn into a serving dish and sprinkle with the chopped chervil. (Serves 4)

Chervil and Haricot (Dried White) Beans

This is often regarded as a winter dish when fresh green beans are scarce, but there is no reason why it should not be made at any time of the year *providing* you have the essential ingredient . . . fresh chervil leaves . . . there is no substitute.

1lb (400g/2$\frac{2}{3}$ cups) haricot (dried white) beans
salt
4oz (100g/$\frac{1}{2}$ cup) butter
4 shallots, finely chopped
2 cloves garlic, crushed
1lb (400g) tomatoes, skinned and chopped
2 teaspoons brown sugar
pepper
2 tablespoons chopped chervil

Soak the beans overnight in cold water. Drain, put into fresh salted water and simmer until tender, about 1$\frac{1}{2}$–2 hours. Drain again. Melt the butter in a large pan, add the shallots and garlic and cook gently for 5 minutes. Add the tomatoes, sugar and seasoning. Simmer for about 5 minutes, then add the hot beans and mix well. Stir in the chervil and serve as soon as possible. (Serves 6)

Broad Beans with Chervil Butter

These beans can also make a course in themselves. Double the quantities in the recipe below and at the last minute add diced, crisply fried bacon.

1lb (400g/2$\frac{2}{3}$ cups) freshly shelled broad beans
salt
1oz (25g/2 tablespoons) butter
2 teaspoons finely chopped chervil
freshly milled black pepper

Cook the beans in boiling salted water until just tender; they will take about 10 minutes if young and fresh, but longer if older. Cream the butter and chervil together and season with plenty of freshly milled black pepper. Drain the beans, put into a serving dish and top with the chervil butter, cut into small pieces. Serve at once. (Serves 4)

Nasturtium Salad with Chervil

1 small lettuce
4oz (100g/1 cup) nasturtium flowers
3 tablespoons olive oil
1$\frac{1}{2}$ tablespoons lemon juice
salt and pepper
1 tablespoon chopped chervil

Wash the lettuce and drain and dry thoroughly. Use to line the outside of a salad bowl. Wash the nasturtium flowers, drain them well and dry on kitchen paper, taking care not to bruise them. Put the oil into a screw-topped jar with the lemon juice and seasoning. Just before serving, shake the dressing well, pour over the flowers and sprinkle with the chopped chervil. (Serves 3–4)

Avocado Pear and Chervil Salad

This can either be served as a starter or as a side salad with a main dish.

2 avocado pears
2 tablespoons lemon juice
1 tablespoon olive oil
salt and freshly milled black pepper
2 tablespoons chopped chervil

Peel the pears, cut into slices and toss in the lemon juice and oil. Season with salt and pepper and put into 1 large or 4 small dishes. Chill, then sprinkle with the chervil just before serving. (Serves 4)

CHIVES

(*Allium schoenoprasum*)

No cook could ask for a more constant ally than chives. Not though, for actual cooking, which, as with chervil, destroys the aroma, but for their remarkable effect on a great variety of cooked dishes and salads.

All through the year they not only submit, but demand a regular 'crew cut' for their delicious leaves and go into a decline if neglected and allowed to produce their pretty purple flowers.

The tiny bulbs of this milder member of the onion family form dense tufts of narrow grassy, tubular leaves, which will grow up to 10 inches (25cm) if allowed, and then be useless as a flavouring. Cut them in succession from the time they are an inch (2·5cm) or so high, down to half an inch (1·25cm) above soil level. This is the masochistic treatment on which they thrive. Pinch out any flower buds which appear and keep the leaves cut back, even if not wanted for the kitchen.

They do most for egg and cheese dishes, salads, soups, particularly vichyssoise, on jacket potatoes, in cream cheese, savoury spreads, cheese sauces and savoury pancakes. The imaginative cook, particularly with a pot of chives ever ready in the kitchen, has to use considerable restraint not to use it as an everyday seasoning.

Cultivation
They are easy to grow in any soil and once you have a clump you will never be without. They generate a highly efficient population explosion underground, and have to be lifted and divided in spring or

autumn after three or four years to prevent overcrowding. Surplus bulbs can be pickled in white vinegar.

Grow them along paths, in the front of flower beds, at the edge of shrubs, in pots, window boxes, in fact anywhere you are not likely to forget their regular trim. Being perennial they slack off in winter and send up new shoots in spring, but by keeping a few pots at different temperatures in the house, you can keep them going most of the winter in colder climates.

Preserving

Chives do not dry well but can be frozen successfully. Wash, scissor or chop them and pack tightly into an ice cube tray. Top with water and freeze. When frozen, turn out into plastic bags and store in the freezer. Take out cubes as required, defrost in a strainer, and use as fresh.

Soups and Sauces

Artichoke Soup

1lb (400g) Jerusalem artichokes
lemon juice (see method)
1oz (25g/2 tablespoons) butter
1 onion, chopped
4 sticks celery, chopped
1 pint (500ml/2½ cups) stock
1 bay leaf
½ pint (250ml/1¼ cups) milk
1 tablespoon cornflour (cornstarch)
salt and pepper
2 tablespoons chopped chives

Peel the artichokes, chop them roughly then put into a bowl of cold water containing a little lemon juice to prevent discolouration. Melt the butter in a pan, add the drained and dried artichokes, onion and celery and cook gently in a covered pan for about 10 minutes. Add the stock and bay leaf, cover and simmer gently for about 35 minutes or until the vegetables are very soft. Either put the vegetables into a liquidizer and blend for 1 minute or put the vegetables through a sieve or vegetable mouli, then blend with the strained stock. Turn the soup back into the saucepan and bring to the boil. Gradually blend the milk into the cornflour (cornstarch) in a basin. When the soup is boiling add the milk and continue to cook, stirring all the time, until the soup has thickened. Taste and adjust the seasoning and serve the soup sprinkled with the chopped chives. (Serves 4)

Chive Sauce (1)

This sauce is a traditional accompaniment to hot boiled beef.

3oz (75g) crustless white bread
milk
2 hard-boiled egg yolks
salt and freshly milled black pepper
¼ teaspoon made mustard
pinch sugar
juice of ¼ lemon
3 tablespoons olive oil
1 tablespoon chopped chives

Put the bread into a basin, cover with cold milk and leave to soak for 5 minutes. Using your hands, squeeze the bread as dry as possible and put into a clean basin. Add the egg yolks and mash with a fork to blend the mixture well. Add the salt, pepper, mustard, sugar and lemon juice, then either sieve the mixture or put it into a blender until smooth. Gradually add the oil, a drop at a time, as if making mayonnaise, until it is all absorbed. Stir in the chives, just before serving. (Serves 4)

Chive Sauce (2)

This sauce is excellent served with grilled (broiled) or fried fish.

3 hard-boiled egg yolks
3 tablespoons salad oil
1 tablespoon vinegar
2 teaspoons chopped chives
salt and freshly milled black pepper

Press the egg yolks through a fine sieve. Very gradually stir in the oil a drop at a time, then beat in the vinegar and chives. Season with salt and pepper. (Serves 4)

Eggs and Cheese

Scrambled Eggs and Brains

2–3 calves' brains
3oz (75g/⅜ cup) butter
2 shallots, finely chopped
6 eggs, beaten
pinch paprika
salt
1 tablespoon chopped parsley
1 tablespoon chopped chives

Soak the brains in cold water for 1 hour, drain and remove as much of the skin and membrane as possible. Put into a saucepan, cover with fresh cold water, bring them slowly to the boil and poach for 1 minute. Drain, then skin and chop. Melt the butter in a pan, add the brains and shallots and cook gently for 5 minutes. Add the eggs and seasoning and cook over a low heat until the eggs are just creamy. Turn on to a serving plate and sprinkle with the parsley and chives. Serve at once. (Serves 4)

Baked Eggs with Chives

2oz (50g/¼ cup) butter
4 eggs
1–2 tablespoons chopped chives
salt and pepper

Divide the butter between 4 ramekin or cocotte dishes. Stand the dishes in a roasting tin containing 1 inch (2·5cm) hot water, put into a moderate oven, 350°F, 180°C, Gas Mark 4 and leave for 10 minutes. Remove from the oven and carefully break an egg into each dish. Sprinkle over the chives and season with salt and pepper. Cover the dishes with foil and bake for 10 minutes or until the whites are just set, but the yolks are still soft. (Serves 4)

Variations: Lightly butter the ramekins only and put a tablespoon of cream in the bottom of each dish. Heat in the dishes and continue as the recipe above.
Use 1 tablespoon chopped chives and 1 tablespoon chopped chervil.
Put a tablespoonful of cooked prawns or shrimps in the bottom of the dishes with cream or butter. Heat in the dishes and continue as the recipe above.

Chive Omelette

Chopped chives are delicious sprinkled over an omelette just before it is folded; allow a tablespoon of chopped chives for a 2–3 egg omelette. If preferred the chives can be mixed with other chopped herbs, such as tarragon and chervil, in which case allow 2 teaspoons of each chopped herb.

Baked Eggs in Tomatoes

This makes a delicious light lunch or supper dish and to make it more substantial you can serve it on rounds of buttered wholemeal toast.

4 large, ripe, firm tomatoes, preferably
    Mediterranean ones
4 tablespoons soft wholemeal breadcrumbs
1 tablespoon chopped basil
1 tablespoon chopped chives
salt and pepper
4 eggs

Cut the tops off the tomatoes. Scoop out the centres carefully with a teaspoon into a bowl and chop finely. Add the breadcrumbs, basil, chives and seasoning to the tomato pulp and mix to a soft paste, adding more breadcrumbs if necessary. Spoon a little of the mixture back into the tomato cases and break an egg into each case. Heap the remaining breadcrumb mixture on top. Bake in a moderate oven, 350°F, 180°C, Gas Mark 4 for about 30 minutes or until the tomatoes are soft, but still hold their shape.

Cream Cheese with Chives

This cheese makes an excellent light lunch served with biscuits or crisp French bread and fruit or it can be served with other cheeses as part of a meal. If you want to make it into a dip to serve with crisps or crudités at a party, add sufficient soured or fresh cream to give a good 'dipping' consistency, i.e. not so stiff that it is difficult to dip into it, but not so soft that it drips.

8oz (200g/1 cup) cream cheese
2–3 tablespoons chopped chives
1 tablespoon chopped parsley
1–2 cloves garlic, crushed
salt and freshly milled black pepper

Turn the cream cheese into a basin and beat in most of the chives, the parsley and garlic and season with salt and plenty of pepper. Turn into a serving bowl and leave for at least 1 hour for the flavours to infuse before serving. Sprinkle with chopped chives before serving. (Serves 4–6)

Turkish Cheese Boreks

8oz (200g) puff pastry or use a 14oz (400g)
  packet frozen puff pastry
8oz (200g) Emmenthal (Swiss) cheese, very
  thinly sliced
1 egg, beaten
6oz (50g/¾ cup) cream cheese
1–2 tablespoons milk
1 tablespoon chopped chives
2 tablespoons chopped parsley
1 clove garlic, crushed
salt and pepper

Roll the pastry out thinly and cut 32 x 3½ inch
(8·75cm) circles. Place 8 of these on a baking
sheet and cover with a slice of cheese, the same
size as the pastry circle. Add a second pastry
circle, dampened with water. Continue these
layers until in each borek you have 4 layers of
pastry and 3 of cheese. Brush the top of each
with beaten egg and bake in a very hot oven,
450°F, 230°C, Gas Mark 8 for about 12
minutes or until the pastry is well risen and
golden brown.
While the pastries are cooking, beat the cheese
with the milk to give a soft consistency, then
blend in the chives, parsley, garlic and seasoning.
Top each pastry with a good spoonful of this
and serve at once. (Serves 4 as a main course or
8 as an hors d'oeuvre)

Vegetables and Salads

Hot Beetroot (Beets) with Chives

1¼lb (600g) baby beetroots (beets)
salt
2oz (50g/¼ cup) butter
1 tablespoon chopped chives
2 teaspoons lemon juice
1 clove garlic, crushed

Wash off the mud from the beetroots (beets)
then cook in boiling salted water for about 1
hour until tender. Strain and rub off the skins
while the beetroot (beets) are still warm. Put
into a heated serving dish and keep warm. Melt
the butter in a small pan, add the chives, lemon
juice and garlic. Mix well and spoon over the
hot beetroot (beets). (Serves 4)

Italian Rice Salad

This is a basic salad which can be varied in
many ways. Prawns, cooked mussels, ham or
chicken can be added. Other vegetables, such
as cucumber and peas can be used as well as, or
in place of those given. It is also a marvellous
way of using up little bits that have been left
over from other meals.

8oz (200g/1⅓ cups) long grain rice
salt
2 tablespoons wine vinegar
4 tablespoons olive oil
pepper
1 small onion, grated
1 green pepper (capsicum), de-seeded and
  chopped
1 red pepper (pimento), de-seeded and
  chopped
3 large tomatoes, skinned, de-seeded and
  chopped
2 sticks celery, chopped
2 tablespoons flaked almonds or pine nuts
2 tablespoons chopped chives

Cook the rice in boiling, salted water until
tender. Drain well and while still warm add the
vinegar, oil, seasoning and onion and toss well.
Add the remaining ingredients when the rice is
cold and mix together. (Serves 4)

Chive Potato Cakes

1½lb (600g) potatoes
salt
2oz (50g/¼ cup) butter
2 tablespoons chopped chives
pepper
1 egg, beaten
little flour
oil or lard for frying

Peel the potatoes and cook in boiling salted
water until tender. Drain, return to the pan and
mash until smooth. Add the butter, chives and
seasoning, mix well then beat in the egg. Allow
the mixture to cool, then shape into flat cakes.
Dust lightly with flour and fry on both sides
until crisp and golden. (Serves 4)

Cucumber and Chive Salad

1 medium-sized cucumber
coarse salt
1 teaspoon tarragon vinegar
1 teaspoon sugar
2 tablespoons single (light) cream
freshly milled black pepper
2 tablespoons olive oil
2 teaspoons chopped chives

Peel the cucumber and cut into wafer thin slices. Put into a colander, sprinkle with coarse salt and leave to drain under a weight for 30 minutes. Mix the vinegar and sugar together in a basin, then add the cream, pepper, oil and chives. Mix well. Place the cucumber in a shallow serving dish and pour over the dressing just before serving. (Serves 4)

Courgette (Zucchini) Salad with Chives

1lb (400g) courgettes (zucchini)
salt
2 tablespoons olive oil
juice of $\frac{1}{2}$ large lemon
freshly milled black pepper
2 tablespoons chopped chives

Wash the courgettes (zucchini) and top and tail them. Cook in boiling salted water for 5 minutes, then drain, rinse in cold water and drain again. Cut obliquely into $\frac{1}{2}$ inch (1·25cm) slices and put into a serving dish. Blend together the oil, lemon juice and seasoning. Pour over the courgettes (zucchini), add the chopped chives and toss well together. (Serves 4–6)

Salade Cevenole

1$\frac{1}{2}$lb (600g) potatoes
salt
1 small head celery
2oz (50g/$\frac{1}{2}$ cup) shelled walnuts, chopped
generous $\frac{1}{4}$ pint (150ml/1 cup) mayonnaise
pepper
1 small curly endive
2 tablespoons chopped chives

Cook the potatoes in boiling salted water until they are just tender. Drain and when cool enough to handle, peel and dice them. Place in a mixing bowl. Chop the celery, discarding the leaves, and add to the potatoes with the walnuts, mayonnaise and seasoning and mix well. Leave until the potatoes are quite cold. Before serving, wash the endive well, dry and place round the outside of a salad bowl. Pile the potato salad into the centre and sprinkle with the chopped chives. (Serves 4–6)

Baked Potatoes with Soured Cream Dressing

4–6 large old potatoes
1 tablespoon oil
$\frac{1}{4}$ pint (125ml/$\frac{5}{8}$ cup) soured cream
1$\frac{1}{2}$ tablespoons chopped chives
1 small clove garlic, crushed (optional)
salt and freshly milled black pepper

Scrub the potatoes, dry well then brush with oil; this helps to crisp the outside skins. Bake in a moderately hot oven, 400°F, 200°C, Gas Mark 6 for 1–1$\frac{1}{2}$ hours, depending on the size of the potatoes. Blend the soured cream with the chives, garlic, if using, and seasoning. Leave to infuse for 15 minutes. Split the potatoes in half and serve topped with the soured cream dressing. (Serves 4–6)

Variation: Add 2oz (50g/$\frac{1}{2}$ cup) crumbled Blue cheese to the dressing

Breads

Cheese Scones

These scones can also be used as a cobbler topping for a casserole. Cook the casserole in the usual way, top with the scones and bake in a moderately hot oven, 375°F, 190°C, Gas Mark 5 for about 20 minutes.

8oz (200g/2 cups) plain (all-purpose) flour
$\frac{1}{2}$ teaspoon salt
1 teaspoon bicarbonate of soda
2 teaspoons cream of tartar
1$\frac{1}{2}$oz (40g/3 tablespoons) butter or
    margarine
2oz (50g/$\frac{1}{2}$ cup) Cheddar cheese, grated
1 teaspoon chopped chives
about $\frac{1}{4}$ pint (125ml/$\frac{5}{8}$ cup) milk

Sift together the flour, salt, bicarbonate of soda and cream of tartar into a bowl. Rub in the butter or margarine until the mixture resembles fine breadcrumbs. Add the cheese and chives and bind with milk to give a soft, but not sticky dough. Turn on to a lightly floured working surface and roll out until it is $\frac{1}{2}$ inch (1·25cm) thick. Cut out 2 inch (5cm) rounds using a pastry cutter. Place on a greased baking tray and bake in a hot oven 425°F, 220°C, Gas Mark 7 for 10 minutes or until risen and golden brown. (Makes 12)

CORIANDER

(Coriandrum sativum)

A slender, erect hardy annual, resembling fennel in appearance, but with a very mixed-up personality. While the treasured ripe seeds emit the most fragrant, alluring scent; the rest of the plant, leaves, flowers and unripe seeds give off a most offensive smell, although the leaves can be used once the seeds have started to ripen.

Coriander seeds however, are used extensively in many cuisines—Continental sausages would not be the same without them, neither would curries, chutneys, stuffings, or marinades, particularly for game. A few crushed seeds add subtle undertones to soups, casseroles, bread, cream cheeses and sprinkled sparingly into cakes and stewed fruits. A most distinct gourmet flavour, it is perhaps at its most impressive in a beetroot salad. It is delicious when rubbed on pork chops or joints of lamb before roasting, and is used in many Moroccan dishes, particularly dried bean soups, which would be unpalatably bland without it.

Cultivation

It grows easily from a spring or autumn sowing and reaches about 2 feet (60cm) with finely cut feathery leaves. The seed stays fertile for at least 5 years. The seed must not be picked till it is absolutely ripe and brown or it will have an unpleasant flavour.

Coriander is not a plant to grow unless you have a passion for curry or other spicy dishes, and disdain the use of bought packets, although it does have a pretty soft mauve flower.

Preserving

Cut off the heads and dry them in an airy shed or similar place on racks over a container lined with cloth or paper or in paper bags. When the seeds are quite dry, shake them out and store in airtight jars; the flavour will improve if they are kept for a month before using.

Hors d'œuvres

Spiced Prawn Pâté

8oz (200g) peeled prawns
6 coriander seeds
1 tablespoon chopped parsley
pinch cayenne pepper
juice of ½ lemon
2 tablespoons olive oil
salt (see method)

Pound the prawns with the coriander, parsley, cayenne pepper and lemon juice in a mortar or put into a blender until smooth. Gradually add the olive oil, a drop at a time, stirring until the mixture is smooth. Taste and adjust the seasoning, adding salt if necessary. Serve with hot toast. (Serves 4–6)

Variation: Use fresh or canned crab meat in place of the prawns in the recipe.

Meat

Portuguese Pork with Lemon

2lb (800g) pork fillet
2 tablespoons olive oil
½ pint (250ml/1¼ cups) dry white wine
4 teaspoons ground cumin
2 cloves garlic, crushed
salt and freshly milled black pepper
6 slices lemon
2 teaspoons coriander seeds, crushed

Cut the meat into 1 inch (2·5cm) cubes. Heat the oil in a pan, add the pork and fry on all sides until the meat is sealed. Add half the wine, the cumin, garlic and seasoning. Bring to the boil, cover and simmer gently for 25 minutes or until the pork is tender. Add the remainder of the wine, the lemon slices, cut into quarters, and the coriander. Cook, uncovered, for a further 5 minutes, and serve with plain boiled rice. (Serves 4—6)

Curried Lamb

1½lb (600g) lean lamb from the shoulder or leg or the fillet
1oz (25g/¼ cup) desiccated (shredded) coconut
¼ pint (125ml/⅝ cup) boiling water
2oz (50g/¼ cup) butter
2 onions, chopped
2 cloves garlic, crushed
1 teaspoon powdered ginger
2 teaspoons coriander seeds
½ teaspoon powdered turmeric
1 fresh chilli, finely chopped
1 teaspoon ground cumin
1½ teaspoons garam masala
2¼oz (56g) can concentrated tomato purée
salt

Cut the meat into neat pieces. Put the coconut into a jug, pour over the boiling water and leave for 10 minutes. Heat the butter in a fireproof casserole and fry the meat with the onions, garlic and spices for 10 minutes, stirring well. Add the tomato purée to the meat together with the strained coconut liquid. Season with salt. Cover and cook in a slow oven, 325°F, 170°C, Gas Mark 3 for 2 hours, stirring from time to time. (Serves 4)

Immos Lamb

This is a Lebanese dish.

generous ¼ pint (150ml/1 cup) water
1 tablespoon olive oil
1½lb (600g) lean lamb from the shoulder or leg
3 onions, sliced
salt and freshly milled black pepper
2 cloves garlic, crushed
2 teaspoons chopped parsley
2 teaspoons cornflour (cornstarch)
1 pint (500ml/2½ cups) natural yogurt
1 teaspoon grated lemon zest
1 tablespoon chopped coriander leaves

Bring the water and oil to the boil. Cut the lamb into 1 inch (2·5cm) cubes. Add to the pan with the onion, salt, pepper, garlic and parsley. Cover and simmer gently for 1½ hours.
Blend the cornflour (cornstarch) with 1 tablespoon water, then beat into the yogurt with the lemon zest. Pour the yogurt into a saucepan and bring slowly to the boil, stirring continuously. Simmer very gently for 10 minutes. Add the yogurt to the lamb and simmer, uncovered for a further 10 minutes. Remove from the heat, taste and adjust the seasoning. Spoon into a serving dish and sprinkle with the chopped coriander before serving. (Serves 4—6)

Kababe Barreh

3lb (1·2 kilo) shoulder of lamb
4 tablespoons wine vinegar
4 tablespoons olive oil
½ teaspoon salt
¼ teaspoon chilli powder
½ teaspoon ground coriander
6 tomatoes
6 onions
2 green peppers (capsicums)
8 mushroom caps

Cut the meat off the bone and cut into 1½ inch (3·75cm) cubes. Put into a shallow dish. Blend together the vinegar, oil, salt, chilli and coriander and pour over the lamb. Leave to marinate for 3 hours, turning from time to time. Drain and reserve the marinade.
Cut the tomatoes into wedges, the onions into quarters and the peppers (capsicums) into 1½ inch (3·75cm) pieces. Thread the meat on to six skewers, alternating with the vegetables. Brush with the marinade and grill (broil) either over a fire or under a gas or electric grill (broiler) for 15 minutes, turning and basting with the marinade. Serve with boiled rice or bread. (Serves 6)

Vegetables and Salads

Ratatouille

2 aubergines (eggplants)
coarse salt
2 onions, finely chopped
4 tablespoons olive oil
2 red or green peppers (capsicums)
4 large tomatoes, skinned and chopped
2 cloves garlic, crushed
12 coriander seeds, crushed
freshly milled black pepper

Chop the unpeeled aubergines (eggplants) into ½ inch (1·25cm) pieces, put into a colander, sprinkle with salt and leave for about 20 minutes for the excess water to drain off. Put the onions into a pan with the oil and cook gently for about 10 minutes or until soft, but not browned. Chop the peppers (capsicums) discarding the cores and seeds and add to the pan with the aubergines (eggplants). Cover and simmer gently for about 20 minutes. Add the tomatoes, garlic, coriander and pepper and continue cooking for a further 15 minutes. Remove from the heat, taste and adjust the seasoning. Serve hot, or allow to cool then chill. (Serves 4—6)

Gobi Ki Sabzi

Indian Spicy Cauliflower

This vegetable dish is also excellent served cold as a salad.

5 tablespoons oil
1 teaspoon mustard seeds
1 inch (2·5cm) piece green ginger, peeled and finely chopped
1 onion, sliced
1 teaspoon turmeric
1 green chilli, finely chopped
1 large cauliflower, separated into florets
salt
juice of ½ lemon
1 tablespoon chopped coriander leaves

Heat the oil, add the mustard seeds, cover and cook for 2 minutes. Add the ginger, onion, turmeric and chilli and cook for a further 3 minutes. Add the cauliflower and salt and mix well. Sprinkle over the lemon juice, cover and simmer gently for 20 minutes. Turn into a serving dish and sprinkle with the chopped coriander before serving. (Serves 4)

Preserves

Spiced Quinces

For this recipe it is important to choose quinces which are only just mature—they must not be over-ripe.

quinces
water
salt
granulated sugar
wine vinegar
coriander seeds

Peel the quinces, cut into quarters and remove the cores. Put into a saucepan, cover with cold water and add a pinch of salt. Bring to the boil and cook gently for 10 minutes. Strain the quinces, measure the water and to each 1 pint (500ml/2½ cups) water add 1lb (400g/2 cups) granulated sugar, ¼ pint (125ml/⅝ cup) wine vinegar and 1 teaspoon coriander seeds. Put into a saucepan, bring to the boil, and stir until the sugar has dissolved. Replace the quinces and cook gently for about 30 minutes or until the quinces are tender. Remove the fruit with a slotted spoon and pack carefully into warm preserving jars. Bring the syrup back to the boil and boil for 2 minutes, then pour over the quinces. Cover and store in a cool, dry place.

Apricot Chutney

1lb (400g) dried apricots
1 large onion, chopped
1¼ tablespoons salt
¼ teaspoon cayenne pepper
4oz (100g/⅔ cup) demerara sugar
4oz (100g/1 cup) sultanas (golden raisins)
1 pint (500ml/2½ cups) distilled malt vinegar
grated zest and juice 1 lemon
2 tablespoons mixed pickling spice
½ teaspoon coriander seeds

Soak the apricots in cold water overnight. Drain and cut each one in half. Put the apricots in a pan with all the ingredients except the pickling spice and coriander. Tie these in a piece of muslin and add to the pan. Cover and simmer for 1 hour. Stir the mixture occasionally so that it does not stick to the pan. Remove the lid and simmer the chutney for a further 20 minutes, stirring frequently. Remove the spices from the pan and pour the chutney into clean, hot jars. Cover with waxed paper and leave to mature for 1 month before using. Makes about 3lb (1·2 kilo).

DILL

(Anethum graveolens)

Enchanting in appearance and flavour, this feathery-leaved annual should be grown by everyone who puts their hearts into cooking. It is slender with feathery, almost threadlike bluish-green leaves, and small deep-yellow flowers in flat saucer heads up to 8 inches (20cm) across. It grows elegantly from $1\frac{1}{2}$–3 feet (45cm–1 metre) and looks remarkably like a refined version of fennel.

Dill has a faint hint of caraway flavour and can act as a stand-in for anyone with an aversion to the latter. It mysteriously combines a cool, refreshing sharpness with slight sweetness. Fennel, if in doubt between the two, has an unmistakable aniseed scent when the leaves are rubbed.

Dill water, an infusion of the dried seeds, has for generations been given to babies to de-wind them and its soothing effect on the digestion has made dill an indispensable ingredient of pickled cucumbers, and such varying foods as chutneys, sauces for vegetables and fish, soups, seafood, sauerkraut, cheese and egg dishes, chicken and meat as well as salads, and in apple pie.

Both leaves and seeds are splendid playthings for serious cooks. The leaves lose their flavour in cooking. The seeds are particularly good in vegetables needing very little water when being cooked, such as shredded cabbage, or crushed onto cauliflower whole if it is being steamed.

Cultivation
Sow the seed in spring where it is to remain and thin the seedlings to 12 inches (30cm). A sunny, sheltered, well-drained border suits them best, where they will be irritated neither by draughts or strong winds. Keep the infant seedlings free of vigorous weeds against which they are too fragile to compete. This does not imply that they are in any way difficult to grow, simply that they may get throttled before you realise they have surfaced.

Warning. Don't sow dill near fennel. The mature plants are so alike that you may get the seeds mixed up when harvesting. Also there is the danger of cross-pollination, so that the following year, the seed may produce neither true dill nor true fennel.

For a continuous supply of young leaves, the seed can be sown from spring to mid-summer, or if the flower heads are not wanted for seed, pinch them out as soon as the buds appear. This treatment, combined with cutting the leaves frequently for use, makes the plants more bushy, rather than like feathery umbrella handles, and keeps their energy producing more leaves.

Dill does not grow well in pots after the seedling stage, nor will it develop seed heads.

Preserving
Leaves to be dried for winter should be cut when still young, spread in a thin layer and put in a dark, warm, airy place till they are brittle. Crumble the leaves from the stems and store in dark, airtight jars. They keep a good colour.

To collect the seeds, pull up the plants or cut them down as the main flowerheads turn brown, but before they become ripe enough to 'spill' out onto the ground. Tie in bunches and hang upside down in a sunny place over a cloth to catch the seeds. When quite dry shake out the seeds and store in airtight containers.

Dill leaves can be preserved in salt. Pick them in the prime of life, discard any tough stalks and chop them roughly. Store in screw-topped jars with a good sprinkle of salt between the layers.

Soups

Quick Tomato and Dill Soup

Dried or fresh dill added to a can of soup can quickly transform it into a gastronomic experience.

10oz (283g) can condensed tomato soup
1 small onion, finely chopped
1 tablespoon chopped fresh or ¼ teaspoon dried dill
4 tablespoons single (light) cream or top of the milk

Empty the contents of the can of soup into a pan and make up according to the instructions on the can. Add the onion and dill and heat gently for 5 minutes. Stir in the cream or top of the milk just before serving with crisp toast. (Serves 4)

Sauces

Dill Seed Sauce

This sauce goes very well with fried, grilled (broiled) or baked fish.

½ pint (250ml/1¼ cups) béchamel sauce (see page 26)
1 tablespoon sherry
1 medium-sized dill-pickled cucumber, sliced
2 teaspoons dill seeds
salt and pepper

Heat the béchamel sauce and stir in the sherry and cucumber. Lightly crush the dill seeds and stir into the sauce. Taste and adjust the seasoning.

Hors d'œuvres

Smoked Mackerel Pâté

2 smoked mackerel
8oz (200g/1 cup) butter, melted

4oz (100g/½ cup) cream cheese
juice of ½ lemon
salt and freshly milled black pepper
1 small clove garlic, crushed
1 tablespoon chopped dill
To garnish:
dill sprigs

Skin and bone the mackerel and either flake and mash finely or put in a blender with the butter. Beat all the remaining ingredients into the mackerel, then turn into a serving dish. Chill for at least 2 hours for the pâté to set and the flavours to infuse. Garnish with sprigs of dill before serving. (Serves 6–8)

Scandinavian Pickled Salmon

This is a very traditional Scandinavian recipe which makes a delicious starter served with buttered rye bread.

1½lb (600g) salmon, from the tail end
2 tablespoons sea salt
1 heaped tablespoon granulated sugar
12 black peppercorns, crushed
1 heaped tablespoon chopped dill
To Garnish:
sprigs of dill
For the Sauce:
3 tablespoons French mustard
1 heaped tablespoon granulated sugar
1 egg yolk
6 tablespoons olive oil
2 tablespoons wine vinegar
2 teaspoons chopped dill
salt and pepper

Ask the fishmonger to fillet the fish into two triangles, or do this yourself. Mix the sea salt, granulated sugar, peppercorns and dill together and spread a quarter of this mixture over the bottom of a flat dish. Lay the first piece of salmon, skin side down, on top of this and spread half the remaining mixture over the cut side. Place the other piece of salmon, skin side up over the first and spread with the remaining mixture, making sure you rub it well into the skin. Cover with foil, then a board with some weights on top. Put into a cool place or refrigerator and leave the salmon for at least 12 hours or up to 5 days, turning occasionally.

To serve the salmon, slice it thinly parallel with the skin, as for smoked salmon, and place on a serving dish. Garnish with sprigs of dill.

Beat the mustard with the sugar and egg yolk until it is smooth and creamy. Gradually add the oil, a drop at a time, then the vinegar and mix well. Add the dill and season with salt and pepper. Serve this sauce separately with the fish. (Serves 6)

Meat

Boiled Lamb with Dill Sauce

Like many other dill recipes, this one comes from Scandinavia and is a good way of serving rather older lamb as the slow cooking makes it very tender.

2lb (800g) best end of neck of lamb
1 tablespoon salt
3–4 peppercorns
1 bay leaf
1 sprig of dill
For the Sauce:
2oz (50g/¼ cup) butter
2oz (50g/½ cup) flour
1 pint (500ml/2½ cups) stock (see method)
3 tablespoons chopped dill
2 tablespoons vinegar
2 teaspoons sugar
1 egg yolk
salt and pepper

Put the lamb into a pan and cover with about 2 pints (1 litre/5 cups) water. Add the seasonings and herbs, bring to the boil, remove any scum, cover and simmer gently for 1–1½ hours until the meat is tender. Melt the butter in a pan, stir in the flour and cook for a minute. Gradually stir in 1 pint (500ml/2½ cups) of stock from cooking the lamb. Bring to the boil, stirring all the time and simmer for 2–3 minutes. Add 2 tablespoons of the dill, the vinegar and sugar. Remove from the heat and stir in the egg yolk and seasoning. Drain the lamb and place on a heated serving dish. Pour over the dill sauce and sprinkle with the remaining dill. (Serves 4)

Desserts

Swedish Apple Cake

2oz (50g/¼ cup) butter
4oz (100g/1⅓ cups) fresh white breadcrumbs
1½lb (600g) cooking apples, peeled and sliced
4 tablespoons water
4oz (100g/½ cup) sugar
1 strip lemon zest
½ teaspoon dill seeds

Melt the butter in a frying pan and fry the crumbs gently until golden brown. If you do not have a very large pan you may have to do this in two batches. Put the apples into a pan with the water, sugar, lemon zest and dill. Cover and cook gently until the apples are reduced to a pulp, then beat well. Put half the apple mixture into the bottom of a greased pie dish, top with half the breadcrumbs, then the apple and then the remaining breadcrumbs. Bake in a moderately hot oven, 375°F, 190°C, Gas Mark 5 for 30 minutes. Allow to cool before serving with cream or a vanilla sauce. (Serves 4)

Preserves

Dill Pickled Cucumbers

about 10 small ridge cucumbers
2 dill flower heads
For the Brine:
4oz (100g/½ cup) salt
1 pint (500ml/2½ cups) water
For the Spiced Vinegar:
¾ pint (375ml/2 cups) cider vinegar
6 peppercorns
2 cloves
1 chilli pepper
6oz (150g/¾ cup) sugar

Put the cucumbers into a bowl. Pour over the salt and water brine and leave for 12 hours. Drain thoroughly, dry well and pack tightly into 1 large or 2 smaller jars with the dill flower heads. Put the vinegar into a saucepan with the peppercorns, cloves and chilli pepper and simmer gently for 15 minutes. Add the sugar, stir until it has dissolved, then strain over the cucumbers. Cover with waxed paper and leave to mature for 1 month before using.
Makes just over 2lb (1 kilo).

50

FENNEL

(Foeniculum vulgare)

A vigorous and graceful perennial which will grow up to 5 feet (1⅔ metres) if left to itself. This, however, is unlikely, as a generous supply of the feathery green leaves is constantly needed for the kitchen. An imposing plant to add dignity to any part of the garden particularly when the flat umbels of yellow flowers, 6 inches (15cm) across, prance above the leaves. The long, flowering stems with their delicate feathery leaves are wonderful cut for the house and last well in water. This helps to keep the plants in order but remember to leave some to go to seed.

Though a native of Mediterranean countries, it has made itself at home in many parts of Europe, growing wild, often in coastal areas, where the fish it enhances, is at its best and freshest.

Both the main stem and vigorous side shoots should be kept picked or cut back to keep the plant productive and under control. It is very like the more refined dill, in early life, both in appearance and cooking uses, but while the short-lived dill has a mild sweet flavour, decidedly its own; fennel is stronger and more robust, with a distinct aniseed flavour, which harmonises particularly well with the more fatty fish, and also makes it more digestible.

The fresh young leaves are a traditional accompaniment for fish, as a stuffing, in a sauce or in the water when fish is poached. It goes equally happily with poultry, liver, kidneys, veal, pork, chopped into soups, salads and vinaigrettes, or sprinkled just before serving onto cabbage, cauliflower, peas, beans and buttered potatoes.

The strongest flavour is in the seed which is pounded when dry and used in cooked apple dishes, sprinkled on fresh fruit, and in cakes, biscuits and bread as well as in savoury dishes. The ripe seed is pleasant to chew, and disguises the less pleasing aftermath of certain foods and drinks. They can also be boiled in water and strained to make a tea, which is good for digestion. Sweetening and milk may be added without upsetting its worthy properties.

Cultivation

Fennel will grow in a variety of conditions but is at its majestic best in a sunny place in well-drained soil which retains moisture without ever becoming sodden. Sow the seed in spring and thin the seedlings to 2 feet (65cm) apart. The plants will need dividing every 3 or 4 years. These take some time to settle down again and will not be as vigorous as new plants, so it is better to transplant and encourage the seedlings which happen around the parent, and discard the old ones when they are obviously on the decline.

It is best not to plant fennel near coriander or caraway in case they get cross-pollinated and it should never be planted near dill. Keep them away too from tomatoes, kohlrabi and dwarf beans which go into a sulk when fennel is a neighbour. On the positive side, fennel, unlike dill, makes a very happy pot or window-box plant if kept cut down to about 12 inches (30cm).

The swollen rooted fennel which is used as a vegetable (Florence fennel or finocchio), popular in France and Italy, demands a long, warm growing period, rich feeding, earthing up and a great amount of water. It does not fatten up well in colder climates and the seed has to be raised in heat early in the year.

Preserving

The leaves, stems and seeds all dry well, though the leaves lose much of their pungency. For the leaves and stems, pick when they are young. Discard any brown or discoloured leaves. Hang in bunches in a warm, dry place, away from strong sunlight, an airing cupboard is ideal. Leave until they are quite dry—the length of time taken to dry them will depend on the temperature and atmosphere of the drying place. When quite dry crumble the leaves into airtight jars and label. Wrap the stems in foil.

For the seed, cut off the flower stems before the ripe seed falls, hang over a cloth in a warm dry place till the seed can be shaken out and store in airtight jars.

If you want to store the leaves for up to two months, pack small bunches in polythene bags straight into the freezer. If you want to keep the herb for a longer period, blanch them in boiling water for 1 minute, drain, dip in cold water, dry well, pack into polythene bags and freeze.

Soups

Summer Bortsch

If you find after cooking the beetroot (beets) for 30 minutes it is not a very good colour, add a little more raw beetroot (beet) to the pan, cook for a further 2—3 minutes, then strain.

1lb (400g) raw beetroot (beets)
2 pints (1 litre/5 cups) stock
1 teaspoon sugar
juice of ½ lemon
salt and pepper
½ teaspoon fennel seeds
2 hard-boiled eggs, quartered
½ cucumber, finely chopped
2 spring onions (scallions), chopped
¼ pint (125ml/⅝ cup) soured cream

Peel the beetroot (beets) and dice into ½ inch (1·25cm) pieces. Put into a saucepan with the stock, bring to the boil and simmer for 30 minutes. Strain the mixture and add the sugar, lemon juice, salt, pepper and fennel seeds. Allow to cool, then chill.

Just before serving add the eggs, cucumber and spring onions (scallions) to the soup. Taste and adjust the seasoning. Turn into 1 large or 4 individual serving bowls and top with the soured cream. (Serves 4)

Hors d'œuvres

Swedish Herring Salad

4 pickled herrings or rollmops
1 dessert apple, cored and sliced
2 teaspoons lemon juice
1 small onion, finely sliced
1 medium-sized cooked beetroot (beet), peeled and diced

8oz (200g) cooked potatoes, diced
¼ pint (125ml/⅝ cup) soured cream
1 tablespoon chopped fennel leaves
salt and pepper
To Garnish:
sprigs of fennel

Cut each herring in half lengthways, then cut each half into 4 strips. Put into a bowl with the apple, add the lemon juice and toss lightly. Add all the remaining ingredients and toss together. Pile into a serving dish and garnish with the fennel sprigs. (Serves 4)

Fish

Baked Cod Steaks with Orange

4 medium-sized cod steaks
juice of ½ lemon
½ teaspoon fennel seeds
salt and freshly milled black pepper
1 orange
1 small onion, thinly sliced
1oz (25g/2 tablespoons) butter

Place the cod steaks in a well buttered ovenproof dish. Sprinkle with the lemon juice and fennel seeds and season with salt and pepper. Peel the orange and cut into 4 slices. Place a slice of orange and some onion rings on each steak and dot with butter. Cover and bake in a moderate oven, 350°F, 180°C, Gas Mark 4 for 15 minutes. (Serves 4)

Sole with Shrimps

8oz (200g) potted shrimps
4 large or 8 small fillets of sole
salt and freshly milled black pepper
2 tablespoons chopped fennel leaves
1 pint (500ml/2½ cups) single (light) cream

Put the shrimps into a saucepan over a very gentle heat until the butter has melted. Strain the butter into a shallow casserole and brush all over the sides. Season the fillets of sole with salt and pepper and divide the shrimps and half the chopped fennel between them. Roll up the fillets and place in the casserole. Pour over the cream and season with more salt and pepper. Cover and cook in a moderately hot oven, 375°F, 190°C, Gas Mark 5 for 20–25 minutes. Serve sprinkled with the remaining chopped fennel. (Serves 4)

Grilled (Broiled) Bass with Fennel

For this recipe it is best to use a double wire gridiron so that it is easy to turn the fish, but if you do not have one, turn the fish over carefully using two fish slices. Alternatively the grilled fish can be placed on a fireproof serving dish with the fennel underneath and lighted at the table with a little brandy poured over.

1 bass, about 3lb (1·2 kilo)
salt and pepper
2 tablespoons olive oil
dried fennel sticks

Clean the fish, season with salt and pepper and brush with olive oil. Put on the oiled rack of a grill (broiler) pan or a gridiron. Put under a moderate grill (broiler) for about 8 minutes, then turn and grill on the other side for about 8 minutes more or until the fish is cooked through. Place some dry fennel sticks in the base of the grill (broiler) pan and set them alight. Leave for a couple of minutes, then turn the fish so that the other side also becomes smoked with the fennel. Serve at once. (Serves 4–6)

Quick Tuna Gratin with Fennel

This dish is easy to make from items in your store-cupboard.

1½oz (40g/3 tablespoons) butter
1 onion, finely chopped
1oz (25g/4 tablespoons) flour
¾ pint (375ml/2 cups) milk
7oz (198g) can tuna
3 teaspoons chopped fennel leaves
salt and freshly milled black pepper
1oz (25g/⅓ cup) fresh white breadcrumbs
1½oz (40g/⅓ cup) Cheddar cheese, grated

Melt the butter in a pan and fry the onion gently for 5 minutes. Blend in the flour and cook for a minute. Gradually stir in the milk and bring to the boil, stirring all the time. Flake the tuna and add to the sauce together with the juice from the can and the fennel. Season to taste with salt and pepper. Turn into an ovenproof dish. Mix the breadcrumbs with the cheese and sprinkle over the top of the fish mixture. Put under the grill (broiler) and grill (broil) for about 5 minutes or until golden brown. (Serves 4)

Poultry and Game

Tuscany Chicken

6 dried fennel sticks
2 large bay leaves
6oz (150g) cooked ham in one piece
3lb (1·2 kilo) roasting chicken
2 cloves garlic, peeled
a strip of lemon zest
½ teaspoon freshly milled black pepper
2oz (50g/¼ cup) butter

Tie the fennel sticks and bay leaves into a bunch and put into the bottom of a casserole. Cut the ham into ½ inch (1·25cm) strips and put inside the bird together with the garlic, lemon zest, pepper and half the butter, cut into small pieces. Spread the bird with the remaining butter and place on its side in the casserole on top of the herbs. Cover and cook in a moderately hot oven, 375°F, 190°C, Gas Mark 5 for 35 minutes. Turn the chicken over to the other side, baste with the butter and cook for a further 35 minutes. Remove the lid, turn the chicken breast upwards, baste and cook uncovered for a further 10—15 minutes or until the chicken is golden brown. (Serves 4—6)

Vegetables and Salads

Hot Coleslaw

1 small white cabbage
salt
6 tablespoons oil
3 tablespoons distilled malt vinegar or cider vinegar
1 teaspoon German mustard
1 tablespoon chopped parsley
½—1 teaspoon fennel seeds
freshly milled black pepper

Shred the cabbage finely and cook in boiling salted water for about 5 minutes or until just tender. Drain well. While the cabbage is cooking, put all the remaining ingredients into a screw-topped jar and shake well together. Turn the cabbage into a serving dish, add the dressing, toss well together and serve at once. (Serves 4—6)

Cucumbers in Cream

1 large cucumber
salt
1oz (25g/2 tablespoons) butter, melted
1 small bunch spring onions (scallions), chopped
1 tablespoon chopped fennel
freshly milled black pepper
4 tablespoons double (heavy) cream

Peel the cucumber, then cut into strips 1 inch (2·5cm) long and ¼ inch (0·75cm) thick. Put into a colander, sprinkle with salt and leave for 30 minutes for the excess water to drain off. Put into a casserole with the butter, spring onions (scallions), fennel and pepper. Cover and cook in a moderate oven, 350°F, 180°C, Gas Mark 4 for 45 minutes. Stir in the cream, taste and adjust the seasoning and cook for a further 5 minutes. (Serves 4)

Note: If you prefer the cucumber and spring onions can be fried gently in the butter for 10 minutes. Stir in the cream, heat gently without boiling and season to taste.

Biscuits (Cookies)

Fennel Biscuits (Cookies)

6oz (150g/¾ cup) butter
6oz (150g/¾ cup) sugar
1 egg yolk
8oz (200g/2 cups) plain (all-purpose) flour
2oz (50g/½ cup) cornflour (cornstarch)
2 teaspoons fennel seeds

Cream together the butter and sugar until light and fluffy, then beat in the egg yolk. Sift the flour and cornflour (cornstarch) together then fold into the mixture with the fennel seeds. Press the mixture into a 7 inch (17·5cm) x 11 inch (27·5cm) greased Swiss roll tin (jelly roll pan). Bake in a moderate oven 350°F, 180°C, Gas Mark 4 for about 30 minutes or until golden brown. Remove from the oven, cool slightly then cut into fingers while still warm. Makes about 12 biscuits (cookies).

Scandinavian Pickled Salmon with Dill and Grilled Bass with Fennel

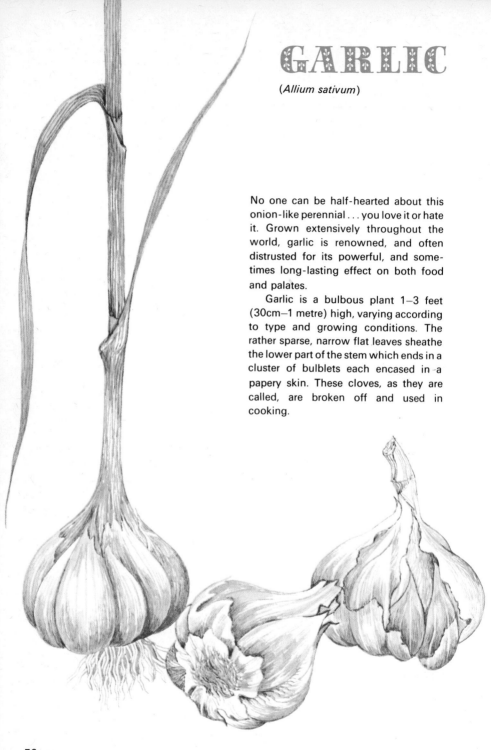

GARLIC

(*Allium sativum*)

No one can be half-hearted about this onion-like perennial . . . you love it or hate it. Grown extensively throughout the world, garlic is renowned, and often distrusted for its powerful, and sometimes long-lasting effect on both food and palates.

Garlic is a bulbous plant 1–3 feet (30cm–1 metre) high, varying according to type and growing conditions. The rather sparse, narrow flat leaves sheathe the lower part of the stem which ends in a cluster of bulblets each encased in a papery skin. These cloves, as they are called, are broken off and used in cooking.

Its uses are infinite and indispensable in all manner of savoury preparations. Some addicted cooks cannot leave it out of anything, until, in time, every dish tastes much the same, the only distinguishing flavour being garlic. Unless used with the greatest finesse, it can be an overwhelming threat to the more delicately distinguished flavours of other ingredients . . . even when merely rubbed round the inside of a salad bowl. It can make or spoil anything it touches. As a solo turn it is at its most subtle in the aioli sauce of Provence, which is served with boiled fish.

Squeeze the juice through a garlic press into sauces, rub on to hot buttered slices of crusty French bread, add to salad dressings. Use whole cloves to stuff chicken, chop and fry with onions, seep whole cloves in olive oil and vinegar to flavour them. In long slow-cooking dishes, garlic has none of the social disadvantages involved in its raw state. Large quantities of it vanish with the utmost tact, imparting their fragrance, and nothing more.

Apart from its wonders in cooking, garlic has long been known as a medicinal herb, for digestion; to clear the blood; spots clear up miraculously after a few days intensive raw garlic eating . . . the disadvantage is that they disappear at the same rate as one's friends. Many European families give their children a clove of garlic to eat each day as a prevention from anything which might go wrong inside or out. It was greatly valued in the Middle Ages for keeping vampires at bay . . . if you consumed enough. In a modern 'Old Wives Tale' context, I have seen and suffered a friend whose hair was coming out in tufts 'alopecia' cured by rubbing raw garlic on the scalp. This was recommended by his barber, the doctor's ointment having had no effect.

Growing

Very easy to grow and cultivate when given plenty of sun and a rich, though light, well-drained soil. They will not even attempt to grow in clay, or a heavy cold soil, and are more likely to rot away than swell.

Separate the cloves and push them into the ground 2 inches (5cm) deep and 6 inches (15cm) apart. Planting time is usually spring in cooler parts of Europe and autumn in warmer climates. The only attention they need is to keep them free of weeds and well watered in dry weather. Pinch out any flower buds which appear. The faded mauve pincushion blooms may be admired by flower arrangers, but are strictly forbidden when the bulb is the main concern.

They will grow in pots and containers only if they are kept well fed and watered and in full sun.

Preserving

When the leaf tops turn brown and dry, lift them and spread in a dry airy place, in sun if possible, to ripen off. Store in a cool dry place on racks in bunches or made into 'ropes'. Keep the best bulbs for replanting the following spring or autumn.

Soups

Garlic Soup

2 tablespoons olive oil
14 cloves garlic
2 pints (1 litre/5 cups) good stock
salt and freshly milled black pepper
2 blades mace

Heat the oil in a pan and gently fry the garlic for about 8 minutes. Pour in the stock and add the salt, pepper and mace. Cover the pan and simmer gently for 15 minutes. Strain the soup into a tureen and serve with crisp toast. (Serves 4)

Sauces

Aioli

This is one of the most famous of all the French Provençal sauces and is often described as the 'butter of Provence'. Traditionally it is always served with cold salt cod and potatoes, but it can be served with any cold fish, meat or salad.

3–4 cloves garlic, crushed
2 egg yolks
freshly milled black pepper
salt
½ pint (250ml/1¼ cups) oil, preferably olive

Put the garlic, egg yolks and seasoning into a bowl and mix well. Using either a balloon whisk or a wooden spoon, gradually add the oil, a drop at a time until you have used about half of it and the mixture looks thick and shiny. At this stage the oil can be added a little quicker until it has all been incorporated. Taste and adjust the seasoning. (Serves 4)

Skordalia

This Greek sauce is generally served with grilled (broiled) fish or with cold raw vegetables.

2 medium-sized potatoes
salt
3 cloves garlic
½ pint (250ml/1¼ cups) olive oil
4 tablespoons vinegar
freshly milled black pepper

Cook the potatoes in boiling salted water until tender. Drain and peel when cool enough to handle. Mash the potatoes very finely. Pound the peeled garlic in a mortar. Add the potatoes and mix well, then gradually add the oil and vinegar alternately, continuing to pound or whisk; the sauce should be thick and smooth like mayonnaise. Season well. (Serves 4–6)

Hors d'œuvres

Patlican Salatsi

Turkish Aubergine (Eggplant) Pâté

2 large aubergines (eggplants)
4 tablespoons olive oil
juice of 1 lemon
1 clove garlic, crushed
salt and pepper
To Garnish:
onion rings

Lightly score the aubergine skins with a knife. Put them on a baking tray and bake in a moderate oven, 350°F, 180°C, Gas Mark 4 for 1¼ hours or until they are completely soft. When they are cool enough to handle, cut them in half and scoop out the pulp. Put this into a bowl and pound or mash until it is fairly smooth. Beat in the oil very gradually then add the lemon juice, garlic and seasoning to taste. Pile into a serving dish and garnish with raw onion rings before serving. (Serves 4–6)

Eggs

Hard-boiled Eggs with Garlic Sauce

10 cloves garlic
2 anchovy fillets
1 teaspoon capers
4 tablespoons olive oil
1 teaspoon vinegar
salt and pepper
6 hard-boiled eggs
2 tablespoons chopped parsley

Peel the garlic cloves, put them into a saucepan of boiling water and cook for 10 minutes. Drain and dry the garlic well, then pound in a mortar with the anchovies and capers until you have a smooth paste. Very gradually beat in the oil, a drop at a time, then finally add the vinegar. Season with pepper, and salt if necessary. Put this sauce into the bottom of a shallow serving dish. Peel the eggs, but leave them whole and arrange on top of the sauce. Sprinkle with parsley before serving. (Serves 4–6)

Pipérade

This dish can be served either hot or cold with croûtons of toast or fried bread.

4 red peppers
4 tablespoons olive oil
1 large onion, finely chopped
2 cloves garlic, crushed
1lb (400g) tomatoes, skinned, de-seeded
    and cut into quarters
8 eggs
salt and freshly milled black pepper

Cut the pepper into ½ inch (1·25cm) pieces, discarding the cores and seeds. Heat the oil in a pan and fry the onion, garlic and peppers gently for 5 minutes. Add the tomatoes and continue cooking for a further 10 minutes. Meanwhile beat the eggs in a basin and season well with salt and pepper. Pour the egg mixture into the saucepan and cook gently over a low heat until the eggs are lightly scrambled. (Serves 4)

Meat and Poultry

Grills (Broils)

For steaks, chops or chicken, either rub a little crushed garlic on to the meat before grilling (broiling), or marinate in a little oil, lemon juice or red or white wine and garlic for 1–2 hours before cooking. Another method of adding garlic is to spread the meat with butter, season with salt and pepper, then lay a few slivers of garlic on top. Grill (broil) the meat in the usual way, then discard the garlic after cooking. This method is also good for fish, such as mullet or mackerel.

Roasts

Joints of beef, veal, lamb and pork are all improved if they are flavoured with garlic before roasting. The garlic can either be crushed and rubbed on to the outside of the joint, or make small slits in the joint and insert fine slivers of garlic into these cuts. For a very mild garlic flavour, just rub the surface of the meat with a cut garlic clove. For chicken and other poultry, either rub crushed garlic into the skin or put two or three peeled cloves inside the bird if it is not being stuffed.

Vegetables and Salads

Garlic in Spinach Purée

In this recipe the garlic flavour is not noticeable in the finished dish, but it has the curious effect of nullifying the iron 'tang' which spinach often leaves on the tongue.

salt
2lb (800g) spinach
4 tablespoons cream
1 clove garlic, crushed
pepper

Heat ¼ inch (0·75cm) salted water in a large saucepan. Add the well washed spinach, cover and cook until the spinach is tender. Drain and sieve or chop finely. Heat the cream in a pan with the garlic and seasoning, without allowing it to boil. Add the spinach and heat until piping hot. Taste and adjust the seasoning and serve at once. (Serves 4)

Garlic Potatoes

The quantity of garlic given in this recipe may seem enormous, but please do not try making it with any less.

2 heads garlic, about 30 cloves
4oz (100g/½ cup) butter
1oz (25g/4 tablespoons) flour
½ pint (250ml/1¼ cups) milk
salt and pepper
2½lb (1 kilo) potatoes
3–4 tablespoons double (heavy) cream
4 tablespoons chopped parsley

Peel the garlic cloves and cook in boiling water for 2 minutes, drain well. Melt half the butter in a pan, add the cloves of garlic and fry gently for 20 minutes or until the garlic is tender. Stir in the flour and cook for 2 minutes, then gradually stir in the milk and bring to the boil, stirring all the time. Season to taste, then either sieve the sauce or put into a blender to make a smooth purée. Cover with a circle of damp greaseproof paper to prevent a skin forming, then put on one side.
Peel the potatoes and cook in boiling salted water until tender. Drain well, then mash with the remaining butter. Gradually beat the garlic sauce into the potatoes, then beat in the cream and most of the parsley. Taste and adjust the seasoning. Spoon into a heated serving dish and sprinkle with the remaining parsley. (Serves 6–8)

Breads

Garlic Bread

This is excellent served with soups, pâtés, mousses or with some of the robust country casseroles, or barbecued meats.

1 medium-sized French stick
3oz (75g/⅜ cup) butter
1–2 cloves garlic, crushed
freshly milled black pepper

Make diagonal cuts in the bread about 1½ inches (3·75cm) apart, but do not go right through to the base. Cream the butter with the garlic and pepper. Spread a good teaspoonful of the butter on to the bread between each cut. Wrap in foil and heat in a very moderate oven, 325°F, 170°C, Gas Mark 3 for about 15 minutes. (Serves 6)

Variation: Garlic and Herb Bread. Add 1 tablespoon chopped parsely and/or 2 teaspoons chopped thyme to the butter.

HYSSOP

(Hyssopus officinalis)

A hardy evergreen, shrubby perennial from the Mediterranean, which grows 18 inches (50cm) high or more with a spread of 9–12 inches (22·5–30cm). The bright blue flowers are continually being fussed over in summer by bees and butterflies, and are a great help in luring cabbage butterflies away from cabbages.

They make an attractive low edging to a flower bed or herb garden if clipped early each spring so that they do not become straggly.

The whole plant is intensely aromatic ... the narrow, dark green leaves as well as the tubular two-lipped flowers, $\frac{1}{2}$ inch (1·25cm) long which open from late summer to autumn. These are enjoyed by flower arrangers as much as bees.

Both leaves and flowers are used as flavouring, which is variously declared to be reminiscent of mint, sage and winter savory. To me, the flavour is that of hyssop. Though the scent is sweet there is an underlying peppery piquancy which scolds the cook who uses it too heavily, with a slight bitterness.

The young leaves and tips of shoots can be picked throughout summer as you need them. They are excellent chopped into salads, stews, soups, stuffings, and impart their distinctive flavour particularly to white sauces. Use the leaves chopped into cottage cheese; with vegetables, especially all kinds of beans; with fish, poultry and meat. It makes an intriguing addition to fruit cocktails and salads, all fruit pies and has a special affinity with cranberries.

Many healing powers were claimed for hyssop by herbalists and physicians.

Tea was made from it to strengthen weak stomachs. A boiled infusion of the leaves was sniffed to relieve catarrh. The boiled leaves and stems were wrapped around aching rheumatic joints, bruises and sprains. Tea made with the dried flowers is renowned for putting vigour into a weak chest. Honey from the flowers is still greatly valued for its delicate, rather than strident flavour.

Cultivation

Sow the seed in spring or autumn in light well-drained soil which does not bear the full force of the sun. Dappled or half shade suits it best. Thin the seedlings to your wishes . . . 12 inches (30cm) apart if you want them to touch, 24 inches (65cm) if you prefer them free-standing.

Hyssop is easy to propagate from 2 inch (5cm) long cuttings of side shoots taken in spring. Pot them into equal parts of peat and sand, and when they have rooted, about early autumn, plant them in their permanent homes. Hyssop should never be sown near radishes as they go into a decline when sown next to it.

Preserving

As hyssop is a perennial evergreen there is little point in drying it, unless for some reason you are unable to reach it during the winter months or you are cutting the plant back to trim it and do not want to waste any. For drying both the leaves and flowers, cut the stems when the plant is bursting with bloom . . . in early morning after the dew has dried. Tie in bunches in a shady, airy place, or lay them on racks. When they are crisp and brittle, separate the leaves and flowers and store them individually in airtight containers.

Soups and Sauces

Hyssop Soup

1oz (25g/2 tablespoons) butter
1lb (400g) potatoes, peeled and finely sliced
1 onion, finely chopped
1½ pints (750ml/3¾ cups) stock
1oz (25g/4 tablespoons) flour
¼ pint (125ml/⅝ cup) milk
1 tablespoon chopped hyssop

Melt the butter in a large pan, add the potatoes and onion, cover and cook gently for 5 minutes. Add the stock, bring to the boil, cover and cook for 30 minutes, or until the vegetables are tender. Blend the flour with the milk. Add ¼ pint (125ml/⅝ cup) of the hot liquid from the pan and blend well. Return to the pan and bring to the boil, stirring all the time. Taste and adjust the seasoning and stir in the chopped hyssop just before serving. (Serves 4)

Cranberry and Raisin Sauce

This sauce goes well with roasted poultry and game, or with hot or cold ham or roast pork.

6oz (150g/¾ cup) sugar
¼ pint (125ml/⅝ cup) water
8oz (200g) cranberries
2 tablespoons seedless raisins
½–1 teaspoon chopped hyssop

Put the sugar and water into a pan and heat gently until the sugar has dissolved. Add the cranberries, raisins and hyssop and cook, uncovered, for 10 minutes or until the cranberries are quite tender. (Serves 4–6)

Hors d'œuvres

Tuna Pâté with Hyssop

7oz (198g) can tuna
1 hard-boiled egg
2 heaped tablespoons cottage cheese, sieved
1 teaspoon chopped hyssop
salt and pepper

Flake the fish and put into a bowl together with the juices from the can. Chop the egg finely and add to the fish with the cottage cheese. Mash well with a fork to blend then stir in the hyssop and season to taste. (Serves 4–6)

Ham and Cheese Spread

This makes a good filling for sandwiches, or can be served as a starter with toast.

8oz (200g) cooked ham, minced (ground)
6oz (150g/¼ cup) cream cheese
4oz (100g/½ cup) softened butter
2 teaspoons chopped hyssop
salt and pepper

Put the ham into a bowl, add the cream cheese and butter and beat well. Stir in the hyssop and season to taste. Pile into a serving dish and chill for 1 hour before serving. (Serves 4)

Savoury Fish with Cheese

4 small fillets of plaice, sole or flounder
salt and pepper
1 shallot, very finely chopped
2 teaspoons chopped hyssop
¼ pint (125ml/⅝ cup) single (light) cream
1oz (25g/¼ cup) Cheddar cheese, grated
1oz (⅓ cup) fresh white breadcrumbs

Season the fish with salt and pepper. Fold in half or roll up and either put each into a ramekin dish or all into one large dish. Add the shallot, hyssop and seasoning to the cream and pour over the fish. Mix the cheese with the bread-crumbs and sprinkle over the top. Bake in a moderately hot oven, 375°F, 190°C, Gas Mark 5 for 20 minutes. (Serves 4)

Poultry and Game

Roast Chicken with Hyssop

For the Stuffing:
4oz (100g/1⅓ cups) fresh white
   breadcrumbs
2oz (50g/¼ cup) butter, melted
1 small onion, grated
salt and freshly milled black pepper
1 teaspoon chopped hyssop
1 egg, beaten
1 tablespoon stock (see method)
For the Chicken:
3lb (1·2 kilo) roasting chicken
1oz (25g/2 tablespoons) butter
1 tablespoon lemon juice
1 teaspoon chopped hyssop
salt and freshly milled black pepper

Put the breadcrumbs into a basin, add the butter, onion, seasoning and hyssop and bind

with the egg. Add the stock if the mixture is too dry. Divide the stuffing between the neck and vent end of the chicken and place in a roasting dish. Spread the chicken with the butter. Pour over the lemon juice and sprinkle with the hyssop and seasoning. Roast in a moderately hot oven, 375°F, 190°C, Gas Mark 5 for 1½ hours, basting from time to time. (Serves 4—6)

Variation: If you do not want to stuff the chicken, simply put a sprig of hyssop inside the bird with a knob of butter and the peeled zest of a lemon to give it added flavour.

Hyssop Pancakes

For the Batter:
4oz (100g/1 cup) plain (all-purpose) flour
pinch salt
1 egg
½ pint (250ml/1¼ cups) milk
1 teaspoon finely chopped hyssop
fat for frying
For the Filling:
2oz (50g/¼ cup) butter
1oz (25g/4 tablespoons) flour
½ pint (250ml/1¼ cups) milk
4oz (100g) button mushrooms, sliced
8oz (200g) cooked chicken, ham or fish,
   chopped
1 teaspoon chopped hyssop
salt and freshly milled black pepper
2 tablespoons grated Parmesan cheese

Sift the flour and salt into a bowl. Add the egg and half the milk and beat to a smooth batter, then beat in the remaining milk and the hyssop. Use the batter to make 8 pancakes. Place the pancakes on a plate and separate each one with a piece of greaseproof paper.
Melt half the butter for the filling in a pan, add the flour and cook for a minute. Gradually stir in the milk and bring to the boil, stirring all the time until the sauce thickens. Add the mush-rooms, chicken, ham or fish, and hyssop. Taste and adjust the seasoning.
Divide the filling between the pancakes, roll up and place in an ovenproof dish. Melt the remaining butter, pour over the pancakes and sprinkle with the cheese. Bake uncovered in a moderately hot oven, 375°F, 190°C, Gas Mark 5 for 20—30 minutes. (Serves 4)

Vegetables and Salads

Mushrooms with Hyssop

6–8oz (150–200g) button mushrooms
6 tablespoons olive oil
1 clove garlic, crushed
1 teaspoon chopped hyssop
salt and freshly milled black pepper
1½ tablespoons lemon juice

Put the mushrooms into a shallow dish. Mix the oil with the garlic, hyssop and seasoning, then pour over the mushrooms. Leave to marinate for about 4 hours. Strain the oil off into a frying pan. Heat, then add the mushrooms and fry until they are golden. Remove from the heat, stir in the lemon juice and serve at once. (Serves 3–4)

Raw Carrot Salad

1lb carrots, peeled and grated
1 small onion, grated
¼ pint (125ml/⅝ cup) natural yogurt
1 teaspoon chopped hyssop
salt and freshly milled black pepper

Put the carrots into a bowl with the onion. Blend the yogurt with the hyssop and seasoning. Spoon over the vegetables and blend well. (Serves 4)

Slimmer's Salad

Cottage cheese is a valuable food for slimmers as it is high in protein and low in calories, but its rather bland flavour can be off-putting. The addition of chopped herbs, hyssop, chives, lovage etc. does much to improve it.

4oz (100g/½ cup) cottage cheese
1 teaspoon chopped hyssop
1 large carrot, grated
1 spring onion (scallion), chopped
½ small green pepper (capsicum), de-seeded
    and chopped
salt and pepper
3–4 lettuce leaves

Put the cottage cheese into a bowl and add the hyssop, carrot, spring onion (scallion), green pepper (capsicum) and seasoning. Blend well. Arrange the lettuce leaves on a serving plate and pile the cottage cheese mixture on top. (Serves 1)

Potato and Apple Salad

1lb (400g) potatoes
salt
1 red-skinned dessert apple
1 tablespoon lemon juice
2 teaspoons chopped hyssop
2oz (50g/½ cup) walnuts, chopped
4–5 tablespoons mayonnaise
1 teaspoon chopped capers
freshly milled black pepper
1 tablespoon chopped parsley

Peel the potatoes and cook in boiling salted water until tender. Drain, allow to cool, then dice. Core the apple, cut into thin slices, then toss in the lemon juice in a bowl. Add the potatoes, hyssop, walnuts, mayonnaise, capers and seasoning and mix well together. Turn into a serving bowl and sprinkle with the parsley before serving. (Serves 4)

Desserts

Apricot and Almond Pie

1lb (400g) apricots
3oz (75g/⅜ cup) sugar
2oz (50g/½ cup) blanched almonds,
    chopped
¼–½ teaspoon chopped hyssop
6oz (150g/1½ cups) plain (all-purpose) flour
pinch salt
3oz (75g/⅜ cup) butter
about 1½ tablespoons water

Halve the apricots and remove the stones (pits). Put into a pie dish and sprinkle with the sugar, almonds and chopped hyssop. Sift together the flour and salt, rub in the butter until the mixture resembles fine breadcrumbs, then bind with water to give a firm dough. Roll out the pastry and cover the top of the pie. Trim and flute the edges. Re-roll the pastry trimmings and cut into leaves or flowers to decorate the top. Bake in a moderately hot oven, 375°F, 190°C, Gas Mark 5 for 35 minutes or until the pastry is golden. (Serves 4)

JUNIPER

(*Juniperus communis*)

A prickly, very hardy, handsome shrub which, when extremely happily married to its soil and situation, has pretentions to become a tree. This, though is only likely to happen on chalky or limey soils, preferably with its back to the wind. In the wild it thrives on hillsides in the most galeswept conditions, with smaller plants sheltering beneath. It should not be confused with the decorative types of juniper which are used for formal plantings.

The shoots of the common juniper bristle with short, needle-like leaves, toning from grey-blue to dark green. The whole shrub, wood, sharp leaves and berries are intensely aromatic. The berries, green at first, take two or three years to ripen and turn blue-black. While these are maturing, new green cones are forming on the bush at the same time, as eventual replacements.

Only the ripe berries are used in cooking, although the oil from the unripe ones is an important ingredient in medicines for digestive and kidney troubles, and in Poland and other countries ham is smoked in juniper. Apart from flavouring gin, the domestic qualities of the berries are invaluable for enhancing dishes with a strong flavour, such as game . . . hare, rabbit, venison, pigeon, quail; and in stuffings for duck, chicken and turkey. They make a distinct difference to pilafs, stews, any robust composite dish and boiled fish. The bitter-sweet astringent flavour of the berries is brought out when they are crushed with a pestle and mortar, or the back of a wooden spoon; 5 to 9 berries should give the right amount of flavour for dishes for four people, using the lesser number in stuffings for delicately flavoured flesh such as chicken. Never be flamboyant with any herb until you have got the measure of it and its different effect in various dishes.

Cultivation

Common juniper is one of the most adaptable evergreen shrubs, whether looking serene and comfortable in an English suburban garden, or stunted and windswept above the tree line in the Alps. It will grow anywhere but thrives best in a chalky or limey soil in the sun. It grows wild in Japan, throughout Asia, Europe and North America.

To produce berries you must make sure you have a female plant, for juniper is a unisexual shrub and it is very rare for both male and female flowers to bloom on a single plant, although you must have a male plant nearby in order to pollinate it. The female flowers are small and rather like cones, while the male flowers are greeny catkins.

The seeds take years to grow into the berrying stage and it is best to buy plants from a nurseryman. Cuttings of young branches put into sandy soil in a cold frame during the autumn, are a little sharper off the mark, but as you are hardly likely to need more than two plants at the most, the initial expense is justifiable.

Preserving

Dry the plump ripe berries gently, separated on trays at room temperature. When they shrivel slightly and have lost any moisture, store in airtight jars.

To keep the absolutely fresh flavour, freeze the newly picked ripe berries in plastic bags as you would currants and raspberries.

Hors d'œuvres

Onions à la Grecque

1lb (400g) button onions
¾ pint (375ml/2 cups) dry white wine
½ pint (250ml/1¼ cups) water
1½oz (40g/3 tablespoons) sugar
3 tablespoons olive oil
8 juniper berries, crushed
juice of 1 small lemon
salt and freshly milled black pepper
1 bay leaf
2¼oz (56g) can concentrated tomato purée
4 sprigs parsley
1 teaspoon chopped basil
To Garnish:
2 tablespoons chopped parsley

Top and tail the onions. Bring a large pan of water to the boil, add the onions and cook for 1 minute. Drain them and peel when they are cool enough to handle. Put all the remaining ingredients into a pan and bring to the boil. Add the onions and simmer gently for 20 minutes or until the onions are tender. Remove the onions with a slotted spoon and place in a serving dish. Boil the liquid in the pan rapidly until it has reduced to three-quarters. Strain over the onions, cool then chill for at least 6 hours in the refrigerator. Sprinkle with chopped parsley before serving. (Serves 4)

Pork and Liver Pâté

1lb (400g) pork belly
1lb (400g) lean veal
8oz (200g) pig's liver
4oz (100g) fat bacon
4 tablespoons dry white wine
2 tablespoons brandy
1 clove garlic, crushed
salt and freshly milled black pepper
6 juniper berries, crushed
¼ teaspoon ground mace

Coarsely mince (grind) the pork, veal, liver and half the bacon. Put into a bowl with the wine, brandy, garlic, seasoning, juniper berries and mace and leave to stand for 2 hours for the flavours to infuse. Pack into a well greased terrine or ovenproof dish and top with the remaining bacon. Cover the terrine and stand in a roasting tin (pan) containing 1 inch (2·5cm) hot water. Bake in a very moderate oven, 325°F, 170°C, Gas Mark 3 for 1½ hours. Remove from the oven, lay a piece of foil over the top and place a weight on this to press the pâté while it is cooling. Allow to become quite cold, then store in the refrigerator. The flavour will be improved if the pâté is kept for 2–3 days before it is used. (Serves 6–8)

Terrine of Hare

To make a terrine of hare, you have to remove all the meat from the bones. This is a fiddly and time-consuming process, but you will find it much easier if you use a fairly small, but very sharp knife.

1 hare
8oz (200g) lean pork
12oz (300g) fat bacon, de-rinded
1 large onion
1 tablespoon chopped parsley
6 juniper berries, crushed
2 teaspoons chopped thyme
2 cloves garlic, crushed
salt and freshly milled black pepper
4 tablespoons red wine
2 tablespoons brandy
4 rashers (slices) streaky (fat) bacon,
    de-rinded

Take all the flesh from the hare off the bones and cut the meat from the back carefully into strips. Put this on one side and mince (grind) the remainder together with the pork, fat bacon and onion. Put into a bowl and add the parsley, juniper, thyme, garlic, seasoning, wine and brandy. Mix well and leave for about 1 hour for the flavours to infuse. Place half the minced mixture in the bottom of a large, well-greased terrine or earthenware casserole. Lay the reserved strips of meat from the back and the bacon rashers (slices) on top, and cover with the remaining minced mixture. Cover with foil and then a lid. Stand in a roasting tin (pan) containing 1 inch (2·5cm) cold water. Cook in a very moderate oven, 325°F., 170°C., Gas Mark 3 for 2½ hours. Remove from the oven, take off the lid and place weights on top of the foil to press the terrine whilst it is cooling. Store

Ingredients for Marinated Pork Chops with Juniper

in a cool place or refrigerator; it is best to keep the terrine for at least a couple of days before serving for the flavours to infuse. (Serves 10)

Variation: Use 2 rabbits in place of the hare.

Meat

Marinated Pork Chops with Juniper

¼ pint (125ml/⅝ cup) red wine
2 tablespoons vinegar
1 carrot, chopped
1 small onion, chopped
1 shallot, chopped
1 clove garlic, crushed
1 bay leaf
a few parsley stalks
1 sprig thyme
4 black peppercorns
6 juniper berries, crushed
1 teaspoon salt
4 thick pork chops
2 tablespoons oil
¼ pint (125ml/⅝ cup) stock
1 tablespoon red currant jelly
juice of ½ orange

Put the wine, vinegar, carrot, onion, shallot, garlic, bay leaf, parsley stalks, thyme, peppercorns, juniper berries and salt into a saucepan. Bring slowly to the boil and simmer for 2–3 minutes, then leave to cool. Put the chops into a shallow dish, pour over the cooled marinade and leave in a cold place for 2 days, turning several times. Heat the oil in a frying pan and fry the chops for about 5 minutes on each side until golden brown. Pour over the strained marinade and the stock and cook gently, uncovered, for about 20 minutes, or until the pork is tender. Remove the meat from the pan, place on a heated serving dish and keep warm. Add the jelly and orange juice to the pan, bring the juices to the boil and boil rapidly for 3 minutes. Pour over the chops and serve. (Serves 4)

German Pork Chops with Plums

4 pork loin chops
12oz (300g) plums
2 tablespoons sugar
2 tablespoons water
4 juniper berries, crushed
¼ teaspoon ground cinnamon
¼ pint (125ml/⅝ cup) red wine
salt and pepper

Put the pork chops into a frying pan without any fat over a low heat. As the fat runs out, increase the heat and cook on both sides until lightly browned. Remove from the pan and place in a casserole. Stone (pit) the plums and put into a saucepan with the sugar, water, juniper and cinnamon. Simmer gently for 15 minutes then either rub through a sieve or put into a blender and make into a smooth purée. Add the wine to the plum purée and season to taste with salt and pepper. Pour over the chops. Cover and cook in a moderate oven, 350°F, 180°C, Gas Mark 4 for 1 hour. Taste and adjust the seasoning before serving. (Serves 4)

Pork Chops with Potatoes

1½lb (600g) potatoes
1 large onion
salt and freshly milled black pepper
2 cloves garlic
4 pork chops
about 8 juniper berries
½oz (15g/1 tablespoon) pork dripping or lard
¼ pint (125ml/⅝ cup) white wine or cider
4 slices of ham or bacon, about 2oz
    (50g) each
2 tablespoons chopped parsley

Peel the potatoes and cut into thin slices. Peel and slice the onion. Put half the potatoes and onions into the bottom of a greased ovenproof dish and season with salt and pepper. Cut the garlic into thin slivers and near the bone of each chop insert a couple of slivers of garlic and a couple of juniper berries. Heat the dripping or lard in a pan and fry the chops quickly on both sides until browned. Remove from the pan and place on top of the potatoes and onions. Cover with the remaining potatoes and onions and season well with salt and pepper. Pour over the wine or cider and cover with the slices of ham or bacon. Cover the dish with foil and then the lid. Cook in a slow oven, 300°F, 150°C, Gas Mark 2 for 3 hours. Remove the dish from the oven, pour off the fat from the meat and sprinkle with the chopped parsley. (Serves 4)

Poultry and Game

Rabbit Casserole

3 tablespoons oil
6 rabbit joints

68

1oz (25g/4 tablespoons) flour
2 tablespoons concentrated tomato purée
$\frac{1}{2}$ pint (250ml/1$\frac{1}{4}$ cups) beef stock
$\frac{1}{4}$ pint (125ml/$\frac{5}{8}$ cup) red wine
1 sprig thyme
2 bay leaves
salt and freshly milled black pepper
8 juniper berries, crushed
1 clove garlic, crushed

Heat the oil in a pan and quickly brown the rabbit pieces on all sides. Remove from the pan and place in a casserole. Add the flour to the fat remaining and cook gently until a golden brown, then add the tomato purée, stock and wine. Bring to the boil, stirring all the time. Add all the remaining ingredients and pour over the rabbit. Cover and cook in a very moderate oven, 325°F, 170°C, Gas Mark 3 for 2 hours or until the rabbit is tender. (Serves 6)

Juniper Stuffed Partridges

6 juniper berries, crushed
6oz (150g) mushrooms, finely chopped
the partridge livers, finely chopped
1oz (25g/2 tablespoons) butter, melted
salt and pepper
a brace of partridge
8 rashers (slices) fat bacon

Put the crushed juniper into a basin with the mushrooms, partridge livers and melted butter. Mix well and season with salt and pepper. Use this mixture to stuff the birds. Wrap two rashers (slices) of bacon round each bird and tie into place with string. Place in a roasting tin (pan) and roast in a moderately hot oven, 400°F, 200°C, Gas Mark 6 for 30-35 minutes, according to the size of the birds. Baste the birds several times during cooking. Serve on large croûtes of fried bread. (Serves 4)

Venison with Juniper

4oz (100g) pork fat
3lb (1·2 kilo) leg or loin of venison, boned
For the Marinade:
1 pint (500ml/2$\frac{1}{2}$ cups) red wine
4 tablespoons olive oil
1 large onion, chopped
12 juniper berries, crushed
1 tablespoon chopped parsley
salt and pepper
For the Sauce:
2oz (50g/$\frac{1}{4}$ cup) butter
2 tablespoons red currant jelly

2 tablespoons lemon juice
$\frac{1}{4}$ pint (125ml/$\frac{5}{8}$ cup) single (light) cream

Cut the pork fat into fine strips and lard the venison with it. Put into a shallow dish. Blend the red wine with the oil, onion, juniper berries, parsley and seasoning and pour over the venison. Leave in a cool place to marinate for 48 hours, turning two or three times a day.
Melt the butter in a fireproof casserole. Add the drained venison and fry until the meat is sealed on all sides. Pour over $\frac{1}{4}$ pint (125ml/$\frac{5}{8}$ cup) of the strained marinade and cover. Cook in a moderately hot oven, 400°F, 200°C, Gas Mark 6 for 2 hours. Remove from the oven, place on a heated serving dish and keep warm. Pour the juices from the pan into a saucepan together with the remainder of the marinade, the red currant jelly and lemon juice. Boil rapidly in an open pan until reduced by half. Remove from the heat and stir in the cream. Return to the heat and heat the sauce gently, without boiling.
Carve the venison into thin slices then arrange on the serving plate. Pour over some of the sauce, and serve the remaining sauce separately. (Serves 6–8)

Vegetables and Salads

Juniper Sauerkraut

This sauerkraut can be cooked on its own to be served with roast pork, grilled pork chops or sausages or you can cook frankfurters, knackwurst or a Polish boiling ring in the pan with the sauerkraut.

15oz (425g) can sauerkraut
2oz (50g/$\frac{1}{4}$ cup) butter
2 rashers (slices) streaky (fat) bacon, de-rinded and chopped
1 large onion, chopped
1 clove garlic, crushed
6 juniper berries, crushed
2 bay leaves
1 teaspoon celery seeds
$\frac{1}{2}$ pint (250ml/1$\frac{1}{4}$ cups) stock

Soak the sauerkraut in cold water for 15 minutes. Drain, then squeeze dry in your hands. Melt the butter in a pan, add the bacon and onion and fry gently for 10 minutes. Add all the remaining ingredients. Cover and simmer gently for 1 hour. Taste and adjust the seasoning before serving. (Serves 4)

LOVAGE

(*Levisticum officinalis*)

A magnificent self-important perennial, reaching up to 6 feet (2 metres) when in flower. It can overwhelm a small herb garden, but as one plant is usually enough to flavour anything an average family could consume in a year, a place must certainly be found for it.

The whole plant has an aura of opulence, with succulent, deeply divided leaves resembling an over boisterous celery. plant. The stately structure is more like that of angelica, with slightly ribbed, hollow stems carrying dense heads of small, yellow-green flowers, followed by oval, brown fruits, which, like most parts of the plant, can be put to use flavouring something.

The leaves taste rather like hot, peppery celery. Roots, seeds and leaves were used widely in herbal medicines to cleanse all corners, nooks and crannies of our internal systems. There seems little that lovage was incapable of improving . . . stomach disorders, fevers, bladder trouble, sore throats and eyes, jaundice and rheumatism . . . prepared in a variety of ways.

Chop the leaves sparingly into salads, so that their robust and slightly harsh flavour does not dominate. You can use a bolder hand when adding lovage to casseroles, stews and soups where its long-lasting flavour comes most into its own. The young stalks as well as the leaves can be cut into 2 inch (5cm) lengths and added to composite dishes or any poultry cooked in liquid. It gives character to somewhat lifeless vegetable and fish soups. Rub fresh, crushed leaves on to any meat before roasting, and put a handful over, under and around while it is cooking.

The crushed seed is used in some Mediterranean countries to spice biscuits, cakes and bread, and the hollow leaf stalks are candied in the same way as angelica, though having a distinctly different flavour.

Cultivation

It is easily raised from seed best sown, if possible, as soon as it is ripe, when it germinates more rapidly, but it will take at least a year before the plant is of a size to start using. The seedlings should be spaced at least 2 feet (65cm) apart. It is quicker to buy a plant or two in spring and start using them immediately in the summer. In later years you can propagate them by dividing the fleshy roots. Cut them into pieces in early spring as the new shoots break through the soil. The roots like to go deep into moist well-worked soil. It becomes a sorry-looking thing in poor, dry conditions. Unless you want to keep the seed for flavouring or to re-sow, the thick flower stalks which come up sturdily from the heart of the plant should be cut down, to encourage new, young leaves.

This is not a plant for the window box, but is just possible in a big pot (at least 14 inches (40cm) diameter) in rich soil, but you will have to give it plenty of water.

Preserving

Use only perfect and young leaves to dry, before the plant flowers. Hang in bunches in a shady, airy place and when completely dry crumble into airtight containers and label.

For the seeds, tie the dead flower heads into bundles, leave in a dry shed or other suitable place over cloths or bags so they can be shaken out when they are completely dry. Store in airtight jars.

The young, hollow side shoots (rather than the coarse main stem) can be candied in the same way as angelica (page 12).

To freeze, wash, scissor or chop the leaves and pack tightly into an ice cube tray. Top with water and freeze. When frozen, turn out into plastic bags and store in the freezer.

Soups

Lovage Soup

1oz (25g/2 tablespoons) butter
2 onions, sliced
2 tablespoons chopped lovage
1oz (25g/4 tablespoons) flour
1 pint (500ml/2½ cups) stock
salt
½ pint (250ml/1¼ cups) milk
pepper, if necessary

Melt the butter and cook the onions gently for 10 minutes, without allowing them to brown. Add the lovage, stir in the flour and cook for a minute. Gradually stir in the stock, season with salt and bring to the boil, stirring all the time. Cover and simmer gently for 15 minutes. Add the milk, heat gently, then taste and adjust the seasoning. (Serves 4)

Sauces

Lovage Sauce

1oz (25g/2 tablespoons) butter
1oz (25g/4 tablespoons) flour

¼ pint (125ml/⅝ cup) milk
¼ pint (125ml/⅝ cup) stock
salt and pepper
1 tablespoon finely chopped lovage

Melt the butter in a pan, add the flour and cook for a minute. Remove from the heat and gradually stir in the milk and stock. Return to the heat and bring to the boil, stirring all the time until the mixture thickens. Season to taste and stir in the chopped lovage. (Serves 4)

Eggs and Cheese

Farmer's Wife Omelette

2 tablespoons oil
2 rashers (slices) bacon, de-rinded and
    chopped
1 large onion, sliced
8oz (200g) cooked potato, diced
2 tomatoes, skinned, de-seeded and
    chopped
2 tablespoons cooked peas
1 tablespoon chopped lovage
salt and freshly milled black pepper
4 eggs
1 tablespoon cold water

Heat the oil in a 7—8 inch (15—17cm) omelette pan and fry the bacon and onion for 10 minutes. Add the potato, tomatoes, peas and lovage and cook for a further 5 minutes. Season with salt and pepper. Beat the eggs with the water and seasoning. Pour over the vegetables and stir, drawing the mixture from the sides to the middle of the pan to allow the uncooked egg to set quickly. Cook until the omelette is just set, then slide on to a serving plate. (Serves 2)

Cheese Pudding

This makes a delicious light lunch and is not as complicated as cooking a soufflé.

4oz (100g/1⅓ cups) fresh white
    breadcrumbs
¾ pint (375ml/2 cups) milk
1oz (25g/2 tablespoons) butter
6oz (150g/1½ cups) Cheddar cheese, grated
3 eggs, well beaten
salt and freshly milled black pepper
1 tablespoon chopped lovage

Put the breadcrumbs into a basin. Heat the milk with the butter, pour over the crumbs and leave for 10 minutes. Add the cheese, eggs, seasoning and lovage. Pour into a buttered, ovenproof dish and bake in a moderately hot oven, 400°F, 200°C, Gas Mark 6 for 30—35 minutes or until well risen and golden brown. (Serves 4)

Meat

Scandinavian Veal Balls

1lb (400g) minced (ground) veal
1 onion, finely chopped
1 tablespoon finely chopped lovage
2oz (50g/⅔ cup) fresh, white breadcrumbs
grated zest and juice ½ lemon
salt and freshly milled black pepper
1 egg, beaten
4 tablespoons single (light) cream
flour
oil for frying

Put the veal into a bowl with the onion, lovage, breadcrumbs, lemon zest and juice and seasoning. Mix well, then bind together with the beaten egg and cream. Put a little flour on your hands to prevent the meat from sticking. Roll the meat into small balls, toss lightly in flour, then fry in hot oil for 5 minutes, turning several times. Serve with lovage sauce (see above). (Serves 4)

Poultry

Braised Guinea Fowl

1oz (25g/2 tablespoons) butter
1 tablespoon olive oil
2 guinea fowl
2—3 lovage stems, finely chopped
¼ pint (125ml/⅝ cup) dry, white wine
¼ pint (125ml/⅝ cup) water
salt and pepper
¼ pint (125ml/⅝ cup) double (heavy) cream

Heat the butter and oil in a large pan and quickly fry the guinea fowl so that they are golden brown all over. Add the lovage, wine, water and seasoning. Cover and simmer gently for 2 hours. Remove the guinea fowl, place on a heated serving dish and keep warm. Boil the liquid in the pan rapidly until it is reduced to a generous ¼ pint (150ml/1 cup), then stir in the cream and heat gently without boiling. Serve this sauce with the guinea fowl. (Serves 6)

Variation: Use a medium-sized roasting chicken in place of the guinea fowl and cook for 1½—2 hours depending on the size.

Vegetables and Salads

Lovage Salad

1 lettuce
¼ cucumber
1 small bunch watercress
4 tomatoes, quartered
1 tablespoon chopped lovage
4 tablespoons olive oil
2 tablespoons lemon juice
pinch dry mustard
pinch sugar
salt and freshly milled black pepper

Wash and dry the lettuce. Peel and thinly slice the cucumber and wash the watercress; discard the stems. Put into a salad bowl with the tomatoes and lovage. Put all the remaining ingredients into a screw-topped jar and shake together until they are well blended. Pour over the salad and toss just before serving. (Serves 4—6)

MARJORAM

Pot Marjoram
(*Origanum onites*)

Sweet or Knotted Marjoram
(*Origanum majorana*)

Wild Marjoram or Oregano
(*Origanum vulgare*)

Marjoram is a native of Asia, Europe and North America, and was used by the Greeks and Romans extensively, both internally and externally. Its reputation for spreading happiness probably goes back to the Middle Ages when it was used abundantly in cooking because of its disinfectant and preserving powers. Like most plants of the *labiatae* family, marjoram aids digestion and has sympathy with troubled stomachs.

A most versatile herb with a sweet spicy flavour. It has a strong personality which can best be exploited with foods which have no pronounced flavour of their own. Use the fresh leaves chopped or whole in ragoûts of pork, veal or with minces. When chopped finely, it is excellent with vegetables, especially spinach, buttered carrots and turnips, potatoes, cabbage, celery, runner beans, salads, soups, fish sauces, cheese and egg dishes.

Pot Marjoram unfortunately contains the least flavour of the three most generally used culinary marjorams, but has the saving grace of being the easiest and most reliable to grow. It is mostly used in company with other herbs and is an important member of a bouquet garni.

A perennial, with erect hairy, reddish stems up to 2 feet (65 cm) high. The dark green leaves are small and inclined to adopt the stem colour and then go browner. The pale pink or white flowers form attractive oblong heads, with an inflorescence much denser than that of wild marjoram, and make the plant a decorative as well as a most useful addition to the flower border.

It has the same uses as the more superior sweet marjoram and can be used as a substitute and grown as a safety bet, when the more tender sweet marjoram fails or is struck down by cold weather. The leaves are less sweet and can sometimes be bitter. The roots have a habit of spreading when particularly contented with their lot. This can be controlled by dividing the clumps when they grow too large.

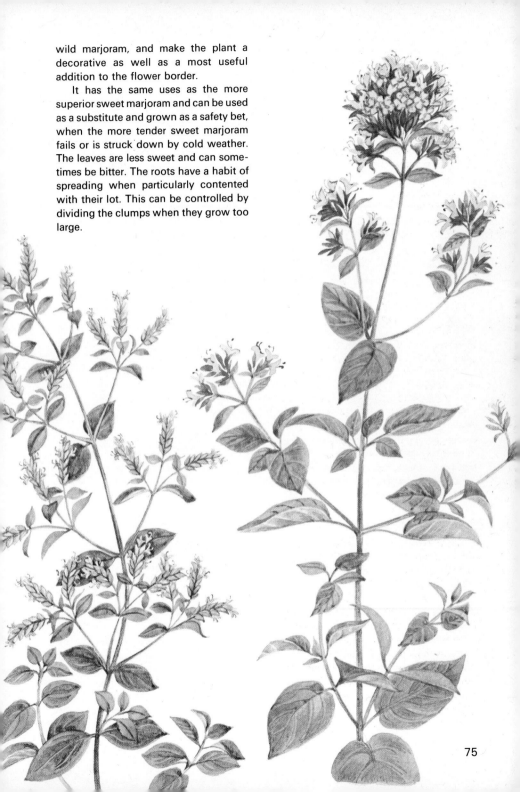

75

Sweet or Knotted Marjoram, is the most aromatic and versatile of all the marjorams, with an alluring, pungent flavour when in league with beef or pork. Good too with fowl, rabbit, in salads and stuffings, black puddings, tripe and kebabs.

It must be treated as a half-hardy in temperate climates as it dies away in winter. In warm climates where the ground never freezes it is perennial.

The flower buds which form during summer and autumn on the sturdy 12 inch (30cm) little bushes, appear in clusters of pearly knots at regular intervals up the stem . . . hence the name. These modest buds and small leaves contain the quite unsuspected magic flavour of the herb. The flowers, white or pale mauve are insignificant and should not be allowed to form. The knotted buds should have been cut on the stems and dried before they open.

Sweet marjoram has a more mild and subtle flavour for most palates than wild marjoram, and can be used in greater quantities without any overwhelming disasters, particularly in meat dishes.

Wild Marjoram or Oregano, gives its distinctive flavour to pizza, spaghetti sauces and other Italian, Spanish and Mexican dishes.

It grows wild on chalky soils, though it can be tamed for garden use. It can be found widely throughout Europe, on chalk downs and hedge banks. It is an erect perennial, which each spring sends up leafy stems growing to $2\frac{1}{2}$ feet (85cm). The species is very variable and the plants in southern Europe are more strongly fragrant than those in cooler climates.

The flavour of dried oregano is immensely strong and penetrating, especially if the flower buds have started to open when it is harvested . . . usually late summer. It dries more quickly than any other herb, probably because of the high concentration of aromatic volatile oils crammed within the leaves, flowers and stems, with the minimum water content.

Because of its power, use oregano with a delicate touch until you test its true strength in different dishes. A really zesty herb for hearty dishes, and it would be unthinkable to make Spaghetti Bolognese or Pizza without it. Its main uses are in all pasta, rice, moussaka, tomato dishes, meat loaf, sausages, and sprinkled on lamb and pork before roasting or grilling.

Growing

All marjorams thrive in light, well-drained soil in full sun, but with shelter from cold winds. Sow seed in spring or autumn, or propagate from cuttings or root divisions in spring.

In cold climates, a winter supply can be kept up by potting plants from the open into sandy soil in late summer, and keeping them in a light, frost-free place. All forms of marjoram can be grown in pots or boxes providing the vigorous root systems are given enough room, and the plants are kept in full sun.

Preserving

Pot marjoram usually keeps some of its leaves in the coldest winters, and is not worth drying. Sweet marjoram is another matter and becomes stronger when dried. Cutting time is vital, varying in different climatic conditions, but always just before the pearly green knotted buds are about to flower. Cut the stems so that some leaves are left behind to send up another crop. For full flavour, cut in the morning after the dew has evaporated. Tie in small bundles and dry in an airy, shady place, or spread out on airy racks in the dark, or in an airing cupboard. When quite dry, crumble the leaves and buds from the stems and store in airtight jars. Dry oregano in the same way.

To freeze marjoram or oregano, pack small bunches in polythene bags straight into the freezer and store for up to 2 months. If you want to keep the herb for a longer period, blanch the branches in boiling water for 1 minute, drain, dip in cold water, dry well, pack into polythene bags and freeze.

Soups

Greek Lamb and Lemon Soup

This is a very filling meat and vegetable soup, a bit like Italian Minestrone. Traditionally it is garnished with finely shredded lettuce heart, but this can be omitted, especially if you are serving it as a warming winter soup. If possible, make this soup the day before you wish to eat it so that it can be cooled down and the solid layer of fat, from the meat, easily removed.

2lb (800g) scrag end of lamb, chopped
2 pints (1 litre/5 cups) water
2 carrots, peeled and sliced
2 small turnips, peeled and chopped
2 onions, chopped
2 leeks, cleaned and sliced
1 stick celery, chopped
1 sprig parsley
2 bay leaves
2 tablespoons chopped marjoram
salt and pepper
2oz (50g/⅓ cup) long grain rice
2 egg yolks
juice of 1 lemon

Trim as much fat as possible off the lamb. Put into a large saucepan with the water and bring to the boil. Remove the scum from the liquid, add the vegetables, herbs and seasoning. Cover and simmer gently for 2½ hours, adding the rice after 1 hour. Discard the bay leaf and parsley, remove the meat, then take all the meat off the bones and chop it. Return to the pan. Remove the pan from the heat and allow it to become quite cold; it is best if you can leave it in the refrigerator overnight. Lift off the layer of solid fat from the top, reheat the soup and bring to the boil. Just before serving beat the egg yolks with the lemon juice in a basin. Add 4 tablespoons of the hot stock, pour back into the soup and heat gently, without allowing it to boil. Serve with pitta or crispy French bread. (Serves 6)

Hors d'œuvres

Chicken Liver Pâté

The flavour of this pâté is improved if it is stored in the refrigerator for about 2 days before serving for the flavours to infuse.

8oz (200g) chicken livers
8oz (200g) sausagemeat
1 egg, beaten
salt and freshly milled black pepper
1 tablespoon chopped marjoram
1 tablespoon brandy
2 tablespoons port
6oz (150g) streaky (fat) bacon rashers (slices)
1 bay leaf

Mince (grind) the livers finely. Put into a bowl with the sausagemeat, egg, seasoning, marjoram, brandy and port. Mix well together. Cut off the rind from the bacon, lay it out on a board, then stretch with the back of a round-bladed knife. Use the rashers to line the bottom and sides of a terrine or ovenproof dish. Spoon in the liver mixture and top with the bay leaf. Cover and stand in a roasting tin (pan) containing 1 inch (2·5cm) hot water. Bake in a moderately hot oven, 400°F, 200°C, Gas Mark 6 for 45 minutes. Allow to cool, then store in the refrigerator. Serve with French bread or toast. (Serves 6)

Potted Ham

This is a very good way of using up left over cooked ham or gammon and once sealed with butter will keep for several days in the refrigerator. Other meats, such as chicken or turkey or leftover game could also be used.

12oz (300g) cooked ham
1 tablespoon chopped marjoram
1 tablespoon brandy or whisky (optional)
salt and freshly milled black pepper
3oz (75g/⅜ cup) unsalted butter

Finely mince (grind) the ham and blend with

the marjoram, brandy or whisky, if using, and seasoning, do not add too much salt if the ham is salt. Melt 2oz (50g/¼ cup) of the butter in a pan. Add the meat mixture and cook gently for 5 minutes. Pack into a jar or pot and leave until cold. Melt the remaining butter in a pan, then strain over the meat to seal it. Store in the refrigerator. (Serves 4)

Aubergines (Eggplants) with Garlic and Bacon

4 medium-sized aubergines (eggplants)
8 rashers (slices) streaky (fat) bacon
2 cloves garlic, crushed
1 tablespoon chopped marjoram
freshly milled black pepper
4 tablespoons olive oil

Make two long slits in each aubergine (eggplant). Cut the rind off the bacon and press a little crushed garlic, some marjoram and pepper into both sides of each rasher (slice). Stuff a rasher (slice) of bacon into each slit and lay the aubergines (eggplants) in a shallow casserole. Pour over the oil, cover and cook in a very moderate oven, 325°F, 170°C, Gas Mark 3 for 2 hours. Remove the cover 30 minutes before the end of cooking time. Serve either hot or cold. (Serves 4)

Fish

Hake with Tomato Sauce

6 hake steaks
salt and freshly milled black pepper
juice of ½ large lemon
3 tablespoons olive oil
1 large onion, chopped
1 clove garlic, crushed
1 small green pepper (capsicum), de-seeded and chopped
1lb (400g) tomatoes, skinned and chopped
2 teaspoons chopped oregano

Put the hake stakes into a buttered ovenproof dish. Season with salt and pepper and pour over the lemon juice and 1 tablespoon of oil. Cover and cook in a moderate oven, 350°F, 180°C, Gas Mark 4 for 25 minutes.
While the fish is cooking heat the remaining oil in a pan. Add the onion, garlic and pepper (capsicum) and fry gently for 5 minutes. Add the tomatoes, seasoning and oregano and simmer for a further 10 minutes. Remove the

fish from the oven and drain off most of the liquid. Pour over the tomato mixture and return to the oven for a further 10 minutes. (Serves 6)

Squid Salad

3lb (1·2 kilo) squid
salt
6 tablespoons olive oil
2 tablespoons vinegar
1 tablespoon lemon juice
3 cloves garlic, crushed
1 tablespoon chopped marjoram
1 tablespoon chopped parsley
freshly milled black pepper
To Garnish:
lemon wedges

Place the squid in the pan with 1 teaspoon salt. Cover with water and bring to the boil. Cover and simmer gently for 35 minutes. Drain, cool, then cut into pieces.
Put the oil, vinegar, lemon juice, garlic, marjoram, parsley and seasoning into a screw-topped jar. Shake well together then pour over the squid. Chill for 30 minutes. Garnish with lemon wedges before serving. (Serves 6)

Variation: Cook the squid as above, but make the dressing with 4 tablespoons mayonnaise, 1 tablespoon lemon juice, 1 tablespoon chopped parsley, 1 tablespoon chopped marjoram, 1 teaspoon chopped capers and seasoning. Pour over the squid and serve as above.

Meat

Catalan Mutton

For the Chick Peas (Garbanzos):
8oz (200g/1⅓ cups) chick peas (garbanzos)
1 onion, sliced
1 clove garlic
1 sage leaf
salt and pepper
For the Lamb:
2 tablespoons oil
8oz (200g) bacon, cut in one piece
3lb (1·2 kilo) lean stewing lamb, jointed
2 cloves garlic, crushed
1 tablespoon concentrated tomato purée
8oz (200g) tomatoes, skinned
1 tablespoon chopped marjoram
1 bay leaf
½ pint (250ml/1¼ cups) white wine
3oz (75g/1 cup) fresh white breadcrumbs

Soak the chick peas (garbanzos) overnight in cold water. Drain, put into a pan, cover with fresh cold water and add the onion, garlic, sage and seasoning. Cover, bring to the boil and simmer very gently for 3 hours or until the peas (garbanzos) are quite tender. Drain.

Heat the oil in a fireproof casserole. Cut the bacon into 1 inch (2·5cm) pieces. Fry the bacon and lamb in the oil until browned on all sides. Add the garlic, tomato purée, tomatoes, marjoram and bay leaf and pour over the wine. Cover and simmer very gently for 2 hours. Taste and adjust the seasoning. Stir in the chick peas, sprinkle with the breadcrumbs and bake uncovered in a very moderate oven, 325°F, 170°C, Gas Mark 3 for 1 hour. (Serves 4–6)

Lamb Cooked in Paper

4 lamb steaks, cut from the leg
3 tablespoons olive oil
juice of 1 lemon
1 tablespoon chopped parsley
1 tablespoon chopped marjoram
salt and pepper
4oz (100g) feta cheese

Put the pieces of lamb into a shallow dish. Combine the oil with the lemon juice, parsley, marjoram and seasoning. Pour over the lamb and leave to marinate for 2–3 hours, turning from time to time. Cut 4 pieces of greaseproof paper large enough to cover the steaks. Put a steak, together with a little of the marinade on to each piece of paper. Cut the cheese into 4 slices and place on top. Wrap up the paper to cover the meat and roast in a moderate oven, 350°F, 180°C, Gas Mark 4 for 1 hour. (Serves 4)

Lasagne al Forno

To leave oregano out of a Bolognese sauce would be like leaving the garlic out of aioli. The Bolognese sauce given in this recipe can be served on its own with spaghetti for Spaghetti Bolognese.

For the Bolognese Sauce:
2 tablespoons oil
4 rashers (4 slices) streaky (fat) bacon, derinded and chopped
1lb (400g) lean minced (ground) beef
3 medium-sized onions, chopped
4 sticks celery, chopped
2 cloves garlic, crushed
1 tablespoon chopped oregano
4 teaspoons salt
1 teaspoon sugar

freshly milled black pepper
5oz (125g) can tomato purée
¾ pint (375ml/2 cups) water
For the Lasagne:
1 tablespoon oil
1 tablespoon salt
12oz (300g) lasagne
1 pint (500ml/2½ cups) béchamel sauce (see page 26)
6oz (150g/1½ cups) Gruyère (Swiss) cheese, grated
2oz (50g/¼ cup) grated Parmesan cheese

Heat the oil in a pan and fry the bacon, beef and onions for 10 minutes, stirring frequently. Add all the remaining ingredients, cover and simmer gently for 1 hour.

Bring a large pan of water to the boil, add the oil and salt. Add the lasagne to the pan, a piece at a time, and cook for 8 minutes. Drain well and rinse in cold water then place on a damp tea towel to dry so that the pieces do not stick together.

Put a layer of the Bolognese sauce in the bottom of a dish, top with a layer of lasagne, then a layer of béchamel sauce and grated Gruyère (Swiss) cheese. Continue these layers, ending with a layer of béchamel sauce. Sprinkle with the remaining Gruyère (Swiss) cheese and Parmesan. Cook in a moderately hot oven 375°F, 190°C, Gas Mark 5 for about 40 minutes or until the top is golden brown. (Serves 8)

Vegetables and Salads

Tomato, Chicory and Grape Salad

6 firm tomatoes
2 large heads chicory
8oz (200g) large, black or white grapes, halved and pipped
2 tablespoons oil
1 tablespoon cider vinegar
pinch dry mustard
pinch sugar
salt and freshly milled black pepper
1 small onion, finely chopped
1 tablespoon chopped marjoram

Skin the tomatoes, cut into quarters and take out the seeds. Cut each head of chicory into 8 pieces lengthways. Put the tomatoes, chicory and grapes into a salad bowl. Put the remaining ingredients into a screw-topped jar. Shake well, pour over the salad and toss well together before serving. (Serves 4–6)

MINT

Spearmint
(*Mentha spicata*)

Apple mint
(*Mentha rotundifolia* — Bowles variety)

Mints are one of the oldest culinary herbs used in Europe, and known to have been grown by the Romans 2000 years ago. Their names and family history though are confusing, as the vast number of different types, and their hybrids are scattered and widespread, and vary, not only in their appearance, but their uses.

I have chosen the two above as being the most useful and aromatic for cooking purposes, but many other kinds have special virtues. Their fresh clean scent has been welcomed into toothpaste, chewing gum, liqueurs, jellies, teas, menthol, chocolate, apart from the universal mint sauce.

The mints most commonly grown for kitchen use, and with good reason are spearmint, with clear green, thin textured narrow leaves, and Bowles variety of apple mint, with large broad fleshy, slightly hairy leaves. Which you prefer is entirely a matter of taste. Bowles is a better long-term grower because it is resistant to rust disease which is liable to attack the leaves and stems of spearmint, and cover them in small orange cups in spring. The shoots have to be pulled up and burnt.

No young peas or potatoes would feel they had been treated as they deserve without some sprigs of mint strewn in them while they are boiling or steaming, with further fresh leaves chopped and sprinkled on top as they are being tossed in butter.

A generous amount of fresh chopped leaves added to any young vegetable just before it is served makes a remarkable

difference, particularly to carrots and turnips. Add them to mushrooms and tomatoes as they are being grilled; into salads, white sauces, and those with a vinegar base. A very nasty practice is to serve a vinegar based mint sauce with roast lamb, if wine is to be drunk; one destroys the other. Much kinder to the palate, as well as the lamb is to have mint jelly or stuff the lamb with a large handful of fresh mint. Or stuff with chopped mint mixed together with breadcrumbs and a grating of lemon peel, or a generous heap of chopped mint with honey and lemon juice. Put a sprig of fresh mint in fruit cups, cocktails and mint juleps.

Cultivation

Mints are vigorous, herbaceous perennials with long, underground runners, which make them bad company for other herbs. They need a bed to themselves. If there is not the space for them to travel, they can be restricted in bottomless metal containers, such as old buckets or water tanks. When several kinds are grown side by side, the more vigorous growers will strangle the weaker ones by root warfare just out of sight in the surface soil. The first you know about it is when you discover you have only one kind of mint instead of two or three. If it happens to be your favourite, there is no problem, otherwise keep the varieties apart.

By choice they are swamp dwellers, but any type of moisture-retaining soil will keep them happy. Their flavour is stronger when they grow in full sun, but this entails the nuisance of watering, and you could not quibble about the loss of flavour when they are in semi-shade.

Before planting mints, have a thought for their height. Spearmint grows about 3 feet (1 metre) high and wide, while Bowles can reach 5 feet (1⅔ metres). The mauve and pink flowers of the various varieties are unobstrusively decorative, but should be cut off, or nipped in the bud, so that the plants will be more

81

concerned to produce more foliage than seed. Only a few mints can be grown from seed, and it is quicker to buy or beg a rhizome. Plant at any time between autumn and spring and increase your stock later by digging up the outer roots, and resetting small pieces in any convenient spot.

As they are so often needed, a well enriched strip between the house wall and a hard path near the kitchen door, will keep mint under control and close to hand. They are not strong enough to rock the foundations. Though the plant dies down during the winter, pots or boxes of the roots can be forced in the house or any warm place throughout the winter.

Preserving

Mint leaves dry well. Pick fresh young leaves, discard any brown or discoloured ones. Hang the leaves in bunches in a warm, dry place, away from strong sunlight. Leave until the leaves are quite dry—the length of time taken to dry them will depend on the temperature and atmosphere of the drying place. When quite dry crumble into airtight jars and label.

To freeze, wash, scissor or chop the leaves and pack tightly into an ice-cube tray. Top with water and freeze. When frozen turn out into plastic bags and store in the freezer. Take out the cubes as required, defrost in a strainer and use as fresh.

Soups

Lebanese Cucumber Soup

1 large cucumber
½ pint (250ml/1¼ cups) single (light) cream
¼ pint (125ml/⅝ cup) yogurt
1 large clove garlic, crushed
2 tablespoons vinegar, preferably tarragon vinegar
2 tablespoons chopped mint
salt and freshly milled black pepper
To Garnish:
sprigs of mint

Do not peel the cucumber, but grate coarsely and put into a bowl. Add the cream, yogurt, garlic, vinegar and mint and season to taste with salt and pepper. Chill for at least 1 hour before serving topped with small sprigs of mint. (Serves 4—6)

Chicken Yogurt Soup

¾ pint (375ml/2 cups) natural yogurt
1½ teaspoons cornflour (cornstarch)
1 tablespoon water
1½ pints (750ml/3¾ cups) good chicken stock
4 large egg yolks
3 tablespoons ground almonds
salt and freshly milled black pepper
1 tablespoon butter
2 tablespoons chopped mint

Pour the yogurt into a saucepan. Blend the cornflour (cornstarch) with the water and gradually beat into the yogurt. Put over a low heat and bring slowly to the boil, stirring all the time. Allow the yogurt to simmer gently for 10 minutes or until it has thickened. In a separate pan heat the chicken stock to boiling point. Blend the egg yolks in a basin and add about ¼ pint (125ml/⅝ cup) of the hot stock. Pour back into the saucepan and put over a very gentle heat stirring all the time until the soup has thickened. On no account must the soup boil or the eggs will curdle. Gradually stir the yogurt into the soup, then blend in the almonds and taste and adjust the seasoning. Just before serving, heat the butter in a small pan and fry the mint for 1—2 minutes, stir into the hot soup. (Serves 6)

Iranian Prune Soup

8oz (200g) prunes
1 large onion, chopped
2 tablespoons long grain rice
2 tablespoons chopped parsley
2 tablespoons chopped mint
4oz (100g/½ cup) lentils
2 pints (1 litre/5 cups) chicken stock
2 pints (1 litre/5 cups) water
1½ teaspoons salt
½ teaspoon black pepper

Soak the prunes overnight, then drain, stone

(pit) and chop. Combine all the ingredients in a large pan. Bring to the boil. Reduce the heat, cover the pan and simmer for 2 hours. Remove from the heat and serve. (Serves 6)

Sauces

Jeryik

This sauce is excellent served with kebabs or roast lamb.

¼ pint (125ml/⅝ cup) yogurt
salt and freshly milled black pepper
2 cloves garlic, crushed
1 tablespoon chopped mint

Blend all the ingredients together and season to taste. Allow to stand for 15 minutes for the flavours to infuse before serving. (Serves 4)

Mint Butter

Either spread this butter on lamb chops before grilling (broiling) or top the cooked chops with knobs of the butter.

2oz (50g/¼ cup) butter
2 tablespoons chopped mint
2 teaspoons lemon juice
salt and freshly milled black pepper

Cream the butter, add the mint, lemon juice and seasoning and beat well. (Serves 4)

Meat

Crusty Roast Lamb

Ideally this lamb should be barbecued over an open charcoal or wood fire, but it is still very good roasted in the oven.

6 cloves garlic, crushed
6 tablespoons fresh white breadcrumbs
6 tablespoons finely chopped mint
2oz (50g/¼ cup) butter
juice of 1 lemon
salt and freshly milled black pepper
4lb (1·75 kilo) leg of lamb

Pound the garlic, breadcrumbs, mint, butter, lemon juice and seasoning to a paste. Spread all over the outside of the lamb, pressing it well in so that it does not fall off during cooking. Leave to stand for 1 hour for the flavours to infuse. Put into a roasting tin (pan) and roast in a moderately hot oven, 375°F, 190°C, Gas Mark 5 for 1 hour 40 minutes, basting several times during cooking. (Serves 8)

Mint Stuffed Lamb

For this recipe, it is important to use mint with long stems as you will see in the method

1 large bunch mint
3lb (1·2 kilo) leg of lamb, boned
1oz (25g/2 tablespoons) butter
salt and pepper

Wash the mint well, but keep it tightly in a bunch. Push the stalks of the mint into the hole where the bone was removed at the shank end. Keep pushing the stalks until they re-appear at the other end then pull them through firmly until the leaves are at the wide end. Cut off the stalks using a sharp knife or scissors. Spread the lamb all over with the butter and season with salt and pepper. Place in a roasting tin (pan) and roast in a moderately hot oven, 375°F, 190°C, Gas Mark 5 for 1½ hours, basting from time to time during cooking. (Serves 6)

Kadin Budu
(Turkish Meat Balls)

3 eggs
1 small onion, finely chopped or grated
1lb (400g) minced (ground) lamb or beef
1 tablespoon long grain rice
1 teaspoon olive oil
1 tablespoon chopped parsley
1 tablespoon chopped mint
salt and freshly milled black pepper
¼ pint (125ml/⅝ cup) water
2 tablespoons milk
2oz (50g/¼ cup) butter

Beat two of the eggs. Put the onion, meat, rice, oil, parsley, mint and seasoning into a bowl. Mix well and bind with the two eggs. Form into 12 balls. Place in a shallow saucepan or frying pan with a lid and pour over the water. Cover and simmer over a low heat for about 40 minutes or until all the water has evaporated. Allow the balls to cool sufficiently to handle and discard any scum. Beat the remaining egg with the milk. Melt the butter in a frying pan. Dip the meat balls in the egg and then fry in the butter until golden brown. Serve with plain boiled or saffron rice. (Serves 4)

Vegetables and Salads

Carrots with Rice and Mint

This is a rather unusual Middle Eastern dish.

1lb (400g) baby carrots
2 tablespoons oil
2 tablespoons long grain rice
salt and pepper
2 tablespoons chopped mint
1 tablespoon lemon juice

Scrape the carrots, cut off the ends and slice in half lengthways. Heat the oil in a pan, add the carrots and cook over a low heat for 2–3 minutes. Stir in the rice, then add enough water to just cover the ingredients. Season with salt and pepper and cook over a low heat for about 20 minutes or until the carrots are tender and the liquid has evaporated. Remove from the heat, stir in the mint and lemon juice and leave to cool. (Serves 4)

Kolokythia Yiachni

Greek Stewed Courgettes (Zucchini)

2lb (800g) small courgettes (zucchini)
generous ¼ pint (150ml/1 cup) olive oil
2 large onions, chopped
1lb (400g) ripe tomatoes
1 teaspoon sugar
¼ pint (125ml/⅝ cup) water
2 teaspoons chopped dill
1 teaspoon chopped mint
salt and freshly milled black pepper

Cut the ends off the courgettes (zucchini), leave them whole if they are very small, otherwise cut them in half. Heat the oil in a pan and gently fry the onions for 5 minutes. Skin the tomatoes and either sieve them or put into a blender to make a smooth purée. Add to the onions with the sugar and cook for 10 minutes. Stir in the water, bring to the boil, add the courgettes (zucchini), herbs and seasoning. Cover and simmer gently for about 40 minutes or until the courgettes (zucchini) are very tender. Taste and adjust the seasoning and serve hot or cold. (Serves 6)

Desserts

Blackcurrant Crumble with Mint

1lb (400g) blackcurrants
2 tablespoons chopped mint
1–2oz (25–50g/2–4 tablespoons) granulated sugar
For the Crumble:
4oz (100g/1 cup) plain (all-purpose) flour
2oz (50g/¼ cup) butter
2oz (50g/¼ cup) granulated sugar
2oz (50g/⅓ cup) soft brown sugar

Wash the currants well, put into a pie dish and stir in the mint and sugar. Sift the flour into a bowl. Cut the butter into small pieces and rub into the flour until the mixture resembles fine breadcrumbs. Add the sugars and mix well. Sprinkle the crumble mixture loosely over the fruit, even it out with a fork, but do not press it down. Bake in a moderately hot oven, 400°F, 200°C, Gas Mark 6 for 30 minutes or until the top is golden brown. (Serves 4)

Variation: Use the mint and blackcurrant mixture to make a fruit pie. Put into a pie dish and top with a short crust or flaky pastry and bake.

Mint Water Ice

¾ pint (375ml/2 cups) water
2 teaspoons (1 envelope) powdered gelatine
6oz (150g/¾ cup) sugar
2 tablespoons chopped mint
2 egg whites

Put 4 tablespoons of the water into a basin and sprinkle over the gelatine. Leave to soften for 5 minutes. Put the sugar and the remaining water into a saucepan. Put over a gentle heat, stirring until the sugar has dissolved, then boil for 5 minutes. Remove from the heat and stir in the gelatine and chopped mint. Stir well and leave for 1 hour for the mint to infuse. Strain into a plastic container or ice cube tray and put into a freezer or ice box of a refrigerator and freeze until the mixture has partly set. Remove from the freezer, turn into a cold basin and whisk until it is opaque. Whisk the egg whites until they form stiff peaks, then fold into the sugar syrup. Freeze for at least 2 hours. (Serves 4)

PARSLEY

(Petroselinum crispum)

One of the universal herbs, known and recognised by the most out of touch gardener, cook, and herb enthusiast, even if only as a garnish. Its greatest disadvantage is that being so familiar, the lazy or unadventurous cook uses it to the exclusion of many other herbs. Even if they eventually find they prefer parsley with everything, only by ringing the changes will this become apparent. As an added bonus it is rich in iron and Vitamin C and renowned for clearing the blood.

Parsley is a slow germinating biennial. First year plants produce much finer and more tender leaves than those in their second year which are about to fulfill their usefulness by producing flowers and seed before going into decline.

The uses of parsley are almost too well known to particularise. The curly variety is best for garnishes, but has little flavour compared with the straight flat and fern-leaved French, Italian and Greek varieties. For long cooking, most of the parsley flavour is in the stalks, hence its addition in a bouquet garni (page 26). Chopped parsley can be used generously in many dishes, but should only be added at the last minute to cooked sauces, omelettes, salads, soups and vinaigrettes. Never let a sauce boil once fresh parsley is added or it will turn green and lose flavour. It is frequently used in conjunction with other herbs, especially chives, tarragon and chervil and their flavours complement one another.

Cultivation

You need patience. Parsley is not a spur of the moment addition to the herb garden. The seed is temperamental and slow to germinate, sometimes refusing to grow in what are considered feather-bed conditions, while self-sown seedlings thrive in most unexpected places.

Parsley likes partially shaded alkaline soil. Sow the seeds where they are to grow from spring until late summer in moderate climates, and thin them to 8 inches (20cm) apart. They can be transplanted in moist warm soil conditions when the seedlings are still small but this often results in their running to seed. The seed takes up to 8 weeks to germinate. Tricks for speeding up this process are to pour boiling water over the seed before the rows are covered, or soaking the seed in water for a few days before sowing.

To keep the leaves producing as long as possible, cut out any flower stems that appear right down to the base. The plants should never be allowed to flower. Always pick the leaves from the outside of the plants, so the young leaves can grow from the heart.

In cold climates when the plants may be damaged by frost, cloches will ensure a continual supply. Alternatively roots can be potted up in autumn before harsh weather and kept watered in the house, a greenhouse or any airy, frost-free light place. It grows well in pots or boxes with enough depth to please the fleshy tap roots.

Preserving

Parsley can be dried but the flavour is better if it is frozen. When the plants are at their most robust and need hard picking to prevent their going to seed, gather large bunches and put immediately into the deep freezer in plastic bags, removing as much air as possible. To use them later, chop before they are completely defrosted, as they lose texture. Any limp stems will flavour soups, stews and stuffings.

87

For short time keeping, close to hand in the kitchen, pull up any crowded roots and keep in a jar of water; keep the stems in water but remember to change the water every day, or put unwashed and dry into a plastic container in the refrigerator.

Sauces

Parsley Sauce

Parsley sauce is generally served with fish, but is also excellent with boiled gammon or bacon, boiled mutton or with broad beans or other vegetables.

1½oz (40g/3 tablespoons) butter
1½oz (40g/6 tablespoons) flour
½ pint (250ml/1¼ cups) milk
¼ pint (125ml/⅝ cup) fish, ham, chicken or
    vegetable stock or use all milk
1½ tablespoons chopped parsley
salt and freshly milled black pepper

Melt the butter in a pan, add the flour and cook for a minute. Remove from the heat and gradually stir in the milk and stock. Return to the heat and bring to the boil, stirring all the time until the sauce thickens. Add the parsley and season to taste; if using ham stock taste the sauce before adding any salt as you may not need any. Do not allow the sauce to boil once the parsley has been added. (Serves 4—6)

Hors d'œuvres

Hummus

8oz (200g/1⅓ cups) chick peas (garbanzos)
salt
juice of 1 lemon
2 cloves garlic, crushed
¼ pint (125ml/⅝ cup) tahina
freshly milled black pepper
2 tablespoons olive oil
2 tablespoons chopped parsley

Soak the chick peas (garbanzos) overnight in cold water. Drain, put into a pan and cover with fresh cold water and 1 teaspoon salt. Cover, bring to the boil and simmer gently for 3 hours. Drain, and reserve the cooking liquor. Either sieve the peas (garbanzos) or put into a blender and make into a smooth purée, then add enough of the cooking liquor to make a smooth paste. Beat in the lemon juice, garlic and tahina, stirring to make a smooth, creamy consistency and season to taste with salt and pepper. Spoon into a serving dish, pour on the olive oil and sprinkle with the parsley. Serve with pitta bread. (Serves 4—6)

Imman Bayildi

The Imman fainted

The legend of this recipe is that the first time it was served to the Imman or Turkish High Priest he thought it was so delicious he fainted with pleasure!

4 medium-sized onions, finely chopped
1 clove garlic, crushed
3 tomatoes, skinned and chopped
3 tablespoons chopped parsley
salt and freshly milled black pepper
4 aubergines (eggplants)
1 pint (500ml/2½ cups) water
1 tablespoon sugar
4 tablespoons olive oil
To Garnish:
1 tablespoon chopped parsley

Put the onions, garlic, tomatoes, parsley and seasoning into a basin and mix well. Using a vegetable peeler, remove four strips of skin from each aubergine (eggplant). Run a sharp knife down each peeled strip to within ½ inch (1·25cm) of each end. Insert the knife blade carefully into the slashes and carefully push the prepared stuffing in with your fingers. Put the aubergines (eggplants) into a saucepan with the water, sugar, oil and seasoning. Cover, bring to the boil and simmer gently for 1½ hours. Allow to cool in the cooking liquor, then remove from the pan and serve sprinkled with fresh parsley. (Serves 4)

Armenian Aubergines (Eggplants)

4 aubergines (eggplants)
coarse salt
4 tablespoons olive oil
1 small onion, finely chopped
1 small red pepper (pimento), de-seeded and
    finely chopped
2 cloves garlic, crushed
8oz (200g) lean minced (ground) lamb
freshly milled black pepper
2 tablespoons chopped parsley
2 tablespoons pine nuts
2oz (50g/⅔ cup) fresh white breadcrumbs

Cut the aubergines (eggplants) in half lengthways. Score the flesh with a knife, sprinkle with salt and leave for 30 minutes for the excess water to drain off. Brush with oil and grill (broil) slowly for about 20 minutes or until tender. Remove the aubergine (eggplant) pulp from the skins and chop it finely. Heat 1 tablespoon of the oil in a pan and fry the onion, pepper (pimento) and garlic for 5 minutes. Add to the aubergine (eggplant) pulp together with the lamb, seasoning, parsley, pine nuts and breadcrumbs. Blend well and pile back into the aubergine (eggplant) shells. Place in an ovenproof dish and sprinkle with the remaining oil. Bake in a moderately hot oven, 400°F, 200°C, Gas Mark 6 for 15 minutes. (Serves 4)

Fish

Kulibyaka

Russian Fish Pie

2oz ($\frac{1}{3}$ cup) long grain rice
salt
2oz (50g/$\frac{1}{4}$ cup) butter
1 small onion, finely chopped
2oz (50g) mushrooms, finely chopped
8oz (200g) puff pastry or use a 14oz (400g) packet frozen puff pastry
2 tablespoons chopped parsley
8oz (200g) cooked fresh salmon or use a 7oz (198g) can of salmon, drained and flaked
2 hard-boiled eggs, sliced
freshly milled black pepper

Cook the rice in boiling salted water for 12 minutes. Drain. Melt half the butter in a pan and fry the onion and mushrooms for 5 minutes. Roll out the pastry and cut into two rectangles 12 inches x 6 inches (30cm x 15cm). Lay one piece of pastry on a baking sheet. Put the ingredients in layers down the centre of the pastry, first the rice, sprinkled with the parsley, then the onion and mushrooms, then salmon and finally the egg slices. Season each layer lightly with salt and pepper. Damp the pastry edges and lay the second piece of pastry over the filling. Seal the edges. Make four slits in the pastry for the steam to escape. Bake in a hot oven, 425°F, 220°C, Gas Mark 7 for 30 minutes. Melt the remaining butter and pour this into the slits in the pie just before serving. (Serves 4)

Poultry

Chicken Kiev

4 chicken breast joints
4oz (100g/$\frac{1}{2}$ cup) butter
2 tablespoons chopped parsley
1 tablespoon chopped chives
1 tablespoon lemon juice
salt and freshly milled black pepper
2 tablespoons seasoned flour
1 egg beaten with 1 tablespoon water
dried breadcrumbs (raspings)
deep fat or oil for frying

Remove the breast bone from each chicken joint, taking great care not to break the flesh of the bird. Skin the chicken breast and cut off the first two bones of the wings. Scrape back the meat from the remaining bone. Put each chicken breast between two sheets of wet greaseproof paper and pound until thin, taking care not to split the meat.
Cream the butter until soft, then beat in the parsley, chives and lemon juice. Divide the butter into four and place on each chicken breast. Season with salt and pepper.
Roll the meat up, envelope fashion, so that the wing bone protrudes, making sure that the butter is well sealed. Toss in seasoned flour, dip in the beaten egg and roll in breadcrumbs. Chill for at least 1 hour.
Heat the oil or fat to 350°F, 180°C, and fry the chicken joints for about 12 minutes. Drain on absorbent paper and serve at once. (Serves 4)

Vegetables and Salads

Parsnips with Onions

4 medium-sized parsnips
salt
2oz (50g/$\frac{1}{4}$ cup) butter
2 medium-sized onions, sliced
1 clove garlic, crushed
2 tablespoons chopped parsley

Peel the parsnips, slice them and cook in boiling salted water for 10–15 minutes or until tender. Drain. Melt the butter in a pan, add the onions and garlic and cook for 5 minutes. Add the parsnips and cook for a further 10 minutes or until the parsnips are brown and crisp. Pile into a heated serving dish and sprinkle with the chopped parsley. (Serves 4)

ROSEMARY

(Rosmarinus officinalis)

Rosemary may well be for remembrance, but it seems remarkably forgotten as one of the most useful and fragrant evergreen shrubs. Folklore abounds with it, yet it remains more common in legends and for the traditions associated with it, than in our gardens.

It is a densely leafy, hardy evergreen shrub, up to 6 feet (2 metres), the short leaves narrow, deep green, almost white on the underside. The strong scent is described variously as a combination of nutmeg, pine needles, ginger, lavender. This complex muddle of associations is easily simplified once you have crushed a sprig of needle-like leaves in your hand. There is nothing like it.

I grow the common rosemary beside house doors so that it is impossible to go in or out without it stroking you, and releasing the heady scent. It is said not to thrive beside a house ruled by a woman. Having watched three well established bushes die on me in quick succession, I anxiously replanted with new cuttings. They thrive, I rule no more or less than before, and I have put down their death to old age.

There are many varieties, some to be seen hugging the barren hillsides of Mediterranean countries, grazed by sheep and goats. All are slow growing, loose if left untrimmed, dense when pruned each year immediately the lavender blue flowers have faded, to encourage new shoots to form and ripen before winter.

Sprigs of rosemary broken from the tips of young shoots, give a wonderful fragrance scattered round lamb, pork, poultry, veal and rabbit while they are roasted or grilled (broiled), and added to any meat stews. The sprigs should be removed when the dish is cooked as they do not soften during the process. To use in a stuffing, or to remain in a dish, cut them up finely with scissors before adding them. They go happily in this state into

marrow dishes, peas, potatoes, soups and fish dishes. Be sparing until you are accustomed to the strength of rosemary.

Its less domestic uses are claimed to be as a hair and scalp tonic; a sprig would improve a glass of beer; and in Greece they boil it and use the water to freshen up black dresses after washing.

Cultivation

Rosemary can be grown from seed if you have the time and patience, but it will be several years before you have a bush large enough to start robbing for the cooking pot. It is more prudent to start with a bought plant, give it a sheltered place, preferably in the sun in well drained limey soil. The plants particularly like house walls, protected from freezing winds. Young plants can put up with more severe weather than older ones.

Where the garden soil is cold, heavy and badly drained, grow rosemary in containers in a sunny corner. They are easily protected with sacking in a severe winter.

When bushes are becoming leggy and starting to die back in parts, they can be readily propagated by tearing off small side shoots with a heel and pushing them into gravelly, sandy soil in the open during the late summer.

Preserving

Since rosemary is an evergreen and provides fresh leaves throughout the year, there is little purpose in preserving it unless you do not want to waste the cuttings when pruning. It dries well; hang the bunches in a cool airy place until they are quite dry then crumble into airtight jars and label.

Fish

Prawns with Rice

2oz (50g/¼ cup) butter
1 small onion, chopped
4 ripe tomatoes, chopped
2 sprigs rosemary
pinch ground cinnamon
salt and pepper
good pinch sugar
1lb (400g) peeled prawns
3 tablespoons dry vermouth
3 tablespoons single (light) cream

Melt the butter in a small pan and fry the onion for 5 minutes. Add the tomatoes, rosemary, cinnamon, seasoning and sugar. Cover and simmer gently for 15 minutes. Either sieve the sauce or remove the sprigs of rosemary and put into a blender. Return to the pan and if the purée is very liquid, boil rapidly for a few minutes until it is reduced and thickened. Add the prawns, vermouth and cream and reheat gently, without boiling. Taste and adjust the seasoning and serve with boiled or Saffron Rice (page 98). (Serves 4—6)

Barbouini

(Fried Red Mullet)

4 red mullet
3 tablespoons flour
salt and freshly milled black pepper
4 tablespoons olive oil
2 sprigs rosemary
4 tablespoons wine vinegar
water (see method)

Clean the mullet, but do not remove the heads or the liver. Season 2 tablespoons of the flour with salt and pepper and coat the fish in this. Heat the oil in a frying pan and fry the mullet on both sides for about 12 minutes or until cooked through. Remove from the pan, place on a heated serving dish and keep warm. Add the rosemary sprigs and the remaining flour to the oil and juices remaining in the pan and cook for a minute. Gradually stir in the vinegar and enough water to give the sauce the consistency of thick cream. Simmer gently for 2—3 minutes, then taste and adjust the seasoning. Remove the rosemary before serving the sauce with the fish. (Serves 4)

Kebab

Meat

Roasts

Traditionally rosemary is always cooked with roast lamb, but it can be used for other meats as well. If cooking with lamb, beef or pork you can either just put sprigs of rosemary on top of the joint and underneath, or make slits in the joint and press a small sprig of rosemary (and a slice of garlic, if wished), into each slit. Roast the joint in the usual way. For chicken, rub the skin of the bird with butter, season and sprinkle with lemon juice and chopped rosemary. Put the peeled zest of half a lemon, a sprig of rosemary and a knob of butter inside the bird and roast in the usual way. Veal can be treated in the same way as lamb, but remember it is a very dry meat, so it is generally better wrapped in foil for the majority of the cooking time. This keeps it moist and also traps in the rosemary flavour.

Grills (Broils)

Rosemary is excellent chopped and sprinkled over lamb chops and cutlets, steaks, pork chops, chicken joints and veal chops before cooking. First spread the meat with butter, or brush with oil, season with salt and pepper and sprinkle with the chopped rosemary. Grill (broil) in the usual way.

Lamb Cutlets en Croûte

2oz (50g/¼ cup) butter
2 teaspoons chopped rosemary
1 clove garlic, crushed
salt and freshly milled black pepper
8 small, lean lamb cutlets
8oz (200g) puff pastry or a 14oz (400g) packet frozen puff pastry
1 egg, beaten

Cream the butter with the rosemary, garlic and seasoning. Spread about a teaspoon of the herb butter on each cutlet and grill on both sides, basting with the butter, until tender. Allow to cool, then spread each cutlet with the remaining butter. Roll out the pastry and cut out 8 rectangles, large enough to completely cover the cutlets. Place a cutlet in the centre. Brush the edges of the pastry with beaten egg, then fold the pastry over so that each cutlet is completely enclosed. Place the cutlets with the joins underneath, on a baking tray. Roll out the trimmings and cut out leaves for decoration. Brush the pastry with beaten egg and bake in a hot oven, 425°F, 220°C, Gas Mark 7 for 20 minutes or until golden brown. (Serves 4)

Kebabs

Shish kebab, shishlik, souvlakia, shashlik, taskebab—all are skewered meat from the Southern Mediterranean countries which are generally cooked over charcoal, although you can grill (broil) them on a domestic cooker. The meat is usually lean lamb cut into cubes and marinated in oil and lemon juice with chopped herbs and often garlic. Sometimes the meat is then just grilled (broiled) on its own or it is put on skewers with vegetables, tomatoes, peppers (capsicums), mushrooms, aubergines (eggplants), courgettes (zucchini), and often with bay leaves as well. The recipe given here is a good basic one which you can vary according to the time of year and the herbs and vegetables you have available.

1lb (400g) lean lamb from the leg
4 tablespoons olive oil
juice of 1 lemon
2 teaspoons finely chopped rosemary
1 bay leaf, crumbled
1 clove garlic, crushed
salt and pepper
3 tomatoes, sliced
1 green pepper (capsicum), de-seeded and cut into 1 inch (2·5cm) squares
1 onion, peeled and cut into eighths
4 mushrooms

Cut the meat into ¾ inch (2cm) cubes and put into a shallow dish. Blend the oil with the lemon juice, chopped rosemary, crumbled bay leaf, garlic and seasoning and pour over the meat. Leave to marinate in a cool place for at least 2 hours. Drain the meat, put on to skewers with the tomatoes, pepper (capsicum) and onion and finish each one with a mushroom. Brush all over with the remainder of the marinade and grill (broil) for about 15 minutes, or until the meat is quite tender, turning frequently. (Serves 4)

Mediterranean Beef Casserole

4 onions, sliced
2 carrots, peeled and sliced
2 cloves garlic, crushed
1 bay leaf
3 sprigs rosemary
1 sprig parsley
2 cloves

salt and pepper
peeled zest of $\frac{1}{2}$ orange
2 teaspoons wine vinegar
$\frac{3}{4}$ pint (375ml/2 cups) red wine
2lb (1·2 kilo) chuck steak
2 rashers (slices) fat bacon
1oz (25g/4 tablespoons) flour
green olives

Put two onions and all the remaining ingredients except the steak, bacon, flour and olives into a shallow dish. Cut the beef into cubes, add to the wine mixture and leave to marinate in a cool place for at least 12 hours or up to 24 hours, turning from time to time. Drain the meat from the marinade and reserve the marinade. Chop the bacon, put into a fireproof casserole and put over a gentle heat until the fat runs. Add the meat and remaining onions and brown the meat on all sides. Add the flour and cook until lightly browned. Stir in the strained marinade. Cover and put into a very moderate oven, 325°F, 170°C, Gas Mark 3 for 2$\frac{1}{2}$ hours. Add the olives to the casserole 1 hour before the end of cooking. Taste and adjust the seasoning before serving. (Serves 4–6)

Pies and Flans

Pissaladière
(Tomato, Olive and Anchovy Flan)

For the Pastry:
6oz (150g) plain (all-purpose) flour
pinch salt
3oz (75g/$\frac{3}{8}$ cup) butter or margarine
about 1$\frac{1}{2}$ tablespoons water
For the Filling:
4 tablespoons olive oil
2 large onions, chopped
1lb (400g) tomatoes, skinned and chopped
1 tablespoon concentrated tomato purée
2 cloves garlic, crushed
1$\frac{1}{2}$ teaspoons chopped rosemary
salt and pepper
2 tablespoons grated Parmesan cheese
1$\frac{3}{4}$oz (50g) can anchovies
black olives

Sift together the flour and salt. Rub in the butter or margarine until the mixture resembles fine breadcrumbs. Bind with water to form a firm dough. Place on a floured surface and knead lightly. Roll out and use to line an 8 inch (20cm) flan ring or tin. Fill the centre with greaseproof paper and baking beans and bake in a moderately hot oven, 400°F, 200°C, Gas Mark 6 for 15 minutes. Remove the greaseproof paper and beans and bake for a further 5 minutes to dry out the base.

Heat the oil in a pan and fry the onions gently for 10 minutes. Add the tomatoes, tomato purée, garlic, rosemary and seasoning. Cover and simmer for about 20 minutes, then cook in an open pan for about 10 minutes, stirring until the mixture is thick.

Sprinkle the base of the flan case with the Parmesan cheese and spoon over the tomato mixture. Cut the anchovy fillets in half lengthways and arrange a lattice over the top of the flan. Brush all over the top of the tomato mixture with oil from the anchovy can. Arrange the olives in the squares of the lattice. Bake in a moderate oven, 350°F, 180°C, Gas Mark 4 for 20–30 minutes or until piping hot. (Serves 4–6)

Vegetables and Salads

Rosemary Baked Potatoes

Scrub medium-sized old potatoes and cut in half lengthways. Sprinkle the cut surfaces with salt and chopped rosemary and place face down on an oiled baking tray. Brush the skins of the potatoes with oil and cook in a moderately hot oven, 400°F, 200°C, Gas Mark 6 for 30–40 minutes. Serve with butter or soured cream.

Rosemary Potato Pie

This potato dish goes very well with roast meats, especially any which are inclined to be dry, and can be cooked in the oven at the same time as the joint.

2lb (800g) potatoes, peeled and sliced
1lb (400g) onions, sliced
salt and freshly milled black pepper
3 teaspoons chopped rosemary
3oz (75g/$\frac{3}{8}$ cup) butter
generous $\frac{1}{4}$ pint (150ml/1 cup) milk

Put layers of potatoes and onions in an ovenproof dish, sprinkling each layer with salt, pepper and chopped rosemary and dotting with small pieces of butter. Finish with a layer of potatoes. Pour over the milk, cover and cook in a moderately hot oven, 375°F, 190°C, Gas Mark 5 for 1$\frac{1}{2}$ hours, removing the lid for the last 30 minutes cooking to brown the potatoes on the top. (Serves 4–6)

SAFFRON

(Crocus sativus)

You are hardly likely to harvest this unique flavouring, even though you can easily grow the plant from which it comes . . . the Saffron crocus, a cultivated form of crocus. The delicate blooms, light purple and mauve, appear in the autumn and are similar to the small flowered spring crocus.

To produce saffron from these delicate flowers takes an army of dedicated gatherers. The blooms are gathered in the early morning just as they are opening in the light. The stigma and part of the style are picked out and dried. It takes about 50,000 blooms to produce 1lb (400g) of saffron . . . which excuses what seems a prohibitive price to buy . . . it is a seasoning to which most of us cannot afford to become addicted.

Saffron Walden, in Essex has long ceased to cultivate the plant and it is now mostly found in Mediterranean countries, particularly Spain, where tiny threads of the dried stigmas are sold in minute packets at the price of gold. Fortunately, a little saffron goes a long way, for nothing can replace it in risotto, fish soup such as the Bouillabaisse of Marseilles, Spanish Paella, curries, breads and cakes.

The riches which Saffron Walden acquired from growing Crocus sativus were mainly from its use as a dye, secondly as a medicine and spice. The industry died out in the eighteenth century when saffron could be imported from hotter countries where it grows more profusely.

To use the threads, crush a few in whatever hot liquid the recipe calls for, and let them infuse for a minute or so. The powder can be sprinkled into any liquid or added to flour.

Soups

Mussel Soup

3 pints (1·5 litres) mussels
2 pints (1 litre/5 cups) water
1 onion, chopped
1–2 bay leaves
salt and freshly milled black pepper
3 tablespoons oil
1 leek (the white part only), chopped
6oz (150g/1 cup) long grain rice
pinch powdered saffron

Scrub the mussels well to remove all the beards and grit. Discard any which are open and do not close when sharply tapped. Put the water into a saucepan with the onion, bay leaves and seasoning. Add the mussels, cover and cook for about 5 minutes or until all the mussels are open. Drain into a sieve and reserve the cooking liquor. Remove the mussels from the shells, put on to a plate and cover with foil or self clinging wrap to prevent them from drying. Heat the oil in a pan and gently fry the leek for 5 minutes. Stir in the rice and toss lightly for a minute or until all the grains are coated with oil. Add the mussel liquor and saffron, cover and simmer for about 15 minutes or until the rice is tender. Add the mussels to the soup a couple of minutes before serving. Taste and adjust the seasoning and serve with crisp Garlic Bread (see page 59). (Serves 6)

Variations: Add 2 skinned, chopped and de-seeded tomatoes with the saffron.
Use vermicelli instead of rice, but reduce the cooking time to 10 minutes.

Mixed Fish Soup

1lb (400g) cod fillet
1 red mullet
1 small mackerel
½ lobster
1 leek, chopped
1 onion, chopped
2 tomatoes, skinned and chopped
2 cloves garlic, crushed
¼ teaspoon powdered saffron
1 bay leaf
2 tablespoons chopped parsley
1 teaspoon salt
freshly milled black pepper
4 tablespoons olive oil
1½ pints (750ml/3¾ cups) water
6oz (150g) peeled prawns

Skin the cod and cut it into 1½ inch (3·75cm) pieces. Bone the mullet and the mackerel and cut into pieces. Break off the claws and legs of the lobster and take out the meat from the claws. Cut the body of the lobster into 1½ inch (3·75cm) pieces, cutting through the shell. Put the leek, onion, tomatoes, garlic, saffron, bay leaf, parsley, salt and pepper into a large saucepan. Pour over the oil and water, cover and bring to the boil. Lower the heat and simmer, uncovered for 10 minutes. Add all the fish, cover and simmer for a further 10 minutes. Serve immediately with plenty of crusty French bread. (Serves 6)

Meat

Veal Chops à la Ampurdanesa

4 veal chops
1 tablespoon butter
1 tablespoon oil
1 onion, chopped
2 tablespoons concentrated tomato purée
¼ pint (125ml/⅝ cup) white wine
¼ pint (125ml/⅝ cup) stock
1oz (25g/¼ cup) mixed blanched almonds
   and hazelnuts
¼ teaspoon powdered saffron
½oz (15g/1 square) bitter chocolate
¼ teaspoon mixed spice
2 tablespoons boiling water
2oz (50g) lean ham
4oz (100g) button mushrooms, sliced
salt and freshly milled black pepper

Fry the chops in the butter and oil in a pan until golden brown on both sides and almost tender. Remove from the pan and place in an oven-proof dish. Add the onion to the fat remaining in the pan and fry gently for 5 minutes. Add the tomato purée, wine and stock and simmer gently for 10 minutes. Grill the nuts until they are golden, then pound in a mortar with the saffron, chocolate and mixed spice. Add the boiling water and mix well, then stir into the wine mixture. Blend well and pour over the cutlets. Cut the ham into fine strips and slice the mushrooms. Place on top of the cutlets and cover the dish tightly. Cook in a moderate oven, 350°F, 180°C, Gas Mark 4 for 45 minutes. Taste and adjust the seasoning before serving. (Serves 4)

Variations: Use joints of rabbit or pork chops in place of veal chops.

Poultry

Sfa Merduma
(Spiced Chicken Casserole)

Traditionally this Moroccan dish is served with cous cous which can be steamed over the chicken, but if you prefer it can be served on plain boiled rice.

3lb (1·2 kilo) chicken
4oz (100g/½ cup) butter
1 teaspoon salt
¼ teaspoon powdered saffron
½ teaspoon freshly milled black pepper
1 teaspoon ground ginger
2 large onions, finely chopped
3 tablespoons chopped parsley
½ teaspoon ground cinnamon
1 tablespoon chopped chervil
2 teaspoons granulated sugar
1 pint (500ml/2½ cups) water

Joint the chicken. Melt the butter in a large pan, add the chicken and fry on all sides until golden. Add all the remaining ingredients, cover and simmer gently for 1½ hours. (Serves 4—6)

Rice Dishes

Saffron Rice

This is served as an accompaniment to an enormous number of varying dishes, such as Osso Buco, curries and kebabs. In the recipe below, white wine is added to the rice, but if you want to be economical this can be replaced with stock.

¼—½ teaspoon powdered saffron
6 tablespoons dry white wine
12oz (300g/2 cups) long grain rice
1½ pints (750ml/3¾ cups) chicken stock
salt and pepper

Stir and dissolve the saffron in the wine. Put into a saucepan with the rice, stock and seasoning. Bring to the boil. Cover and simmer gently for 15 minutes or until the rice is tender and has absorbed all the liquid. (Serves 4—6)

Sayadiah
(Fish Risotto)

2 tablespoons oil
1 large onion, chopped
6oz (150g/1 cup) long grain rice
1 pint (500ml/2½ cups) water
1 red pepper (pimento)
1 green pepper (capsicum)

1lb (400g) halibut, cod or snapper
1 bay leaf
¼ teaspoon powdered saffron
1 teaspoon salt
pepper
2oz (50g) peeled prawns

Heat the oil in a large pan. Add the onion and fry for 5 minutes, stir in the rice and fry for a further 5 minutes. Add the water and bring to the boil. Cut the peppers (pimento and capsicum) into rings, discarding the cores and seeds. Cut the fish into 1 inch (2·5cm) pieces, discarding the bones and skin, and crush the bay leaf. Add to the pan with the saffron and seasoning. Cover and simmer gently for about 20 minutes or until the rice is tender and the liquid is absorbed. Stir in the prawns, taste and adjust the seasoning and serve. (Serves 4)

Saffron Rice Salad with Fish

cooked saffron rice as the recipe above
6 tablespoons olive oil
2 tablespoons wine vinegar
2 cloves garlic, crushed
4 tablespoons chopped parsley
1 teaspoon French mustard
salt and pepper
12oz (300g) cooked haddock or other white fish, flaked
2oz (50g/¼ cup) black olives
To Garnish:
4 tomatoes, sliced

Put the rice into a bowl. Blend together the oil, vinegar, garlic, parsley, mustard and seasoning. Add to the rice while it is still warm, mix well and leave to cool. Add the fish and olives and toss lightly together. Turn into a serving bowl and garnish with the sliced tomatoes.

Variation: Add 8oz (200g) peeled prawns to the salad as well.

Risotto alla Milanese

1 marrow bone
3oz (75g/⅜ cup) butter
1 large onion, chopped
¼ pint (125ml/⅝ cup) dry white wine
1lb (400g/2⅔ cups) Italian rice or long grain rice
2 pints (1 litre/5 cups) beef stock
½ teaspoon powdered saffron
2—3oz (50—75g/¼—⅜ cup) grated Parmesan cheese
salt and pepper

Ask the butcher to chop the bone into several pieces for you so that you can extract the marrow easily—you should have about 2oz (50g).

Melt half the butter in a pan, add the marrow and the onion and fry for 5 minutes. Add the wine and boil rapidly until the wine has reduced by half. Stir in the rice and cook for 2–3 minutes, then pour over the stock and add the saffron. Stir well to blend. Cover and cook over a moderate heat for about 15 minutes, or until the rice is tender and all the liquid has been absorbed. Add the remainder of the butter and the cheese and taste and adjust the seasoning. Serve at once. (Serves 6)

Paella alla Valencia

2 pints (1 litre) fresh mussels
salt and pepper
2 tablespoons olive oil
4 chicken drumsticks
1 large onion, chopped
1 green or red pepper (capsicum or pimento), de-seeded and chopped
6oz (150g/1 cup) long grain rice
¼ teaspoon powdered saffron
4oz (100g) shelled prawns or shrimps
4oz (100g) garlic sausage, sliced
To Garnish:
black olives
4oz (100g) cooked unshelled prawns

Scrub the mussels and remove all the beards. Discard any which are open and do not close when sharply tapped. Put the mussels into a pan with salt, pepper and water to cover. Simmer gently until they open, about 5 minutes. Remove the mussels from their shells, reserving about 8 in their shells for garnish. Retain the cooking liquor. Heat the oil and fry the chicken, onion and pepper (capsicum or pimento) for about 5 minutes. Add the rice and fry for 2 minutes. Make the liquid from the mussels up to ¾ pint (375ml/2 cups) with water and blend in the saffron. Stir in the rice, then simmer gently over a low heat for 20 minutes.

Stir in the shelled prawns, garlic sausage and mussels. Cook for a further 5 minutes, adding a little extra water if it looks too dry. Garnish with the reserved mussels, olives and un-shelled prawns.

Cakes

Saffron Sponge

8oz (200g/2 cups) self-raising flour
¼ teaspoon powdered saffron
¼ teaspoon salt
4oz (100g/½ cup) butter
3oz (75g/⅜ cup) soft brown sugar
2 tablespoons chopped candied peel
2 eggs, beaten
¼ pint (125ml/⅝ cup) milk
¼ pint (125ml/⅝ cup) double (heavy) cream, lightly whipped
sifted icing (confectioners') sugar

Sift together the flour, saffron and salt. Rub in the butter until the mixture resembles fine breadcrumbs, then add the sugar and peel. Bind the dry ingredients with the eggs and milk and turn into a greased and floured 7 inch (17·5cm) cake tin (pan). Bake in a moderately hot oven, 375°F, 190°C, Gas Mark 5 for about 25 minutes. Turn out of the tin (pan) on to a wire rack and leave to cool. Split the cake in half and fill with the whipped cream. Dust with icing (confectioners') sugar before serving.

Saffron Cake

scant ½oz (15g) yeast
½ pint (250ml/1¼ cups) warm water
1lb (800g/4 cups) plain (all purpose) flour
½ teaspoon salt
good pinch powdered saffron
8oz (200g/1 cup) butter
4oz (100g/½ cup) caster (granulated) sugar
2 eggs, beaten
6oz (150g/1 cup) seedless raisins

Cream the yeast and add the warm water. Stir into it enough sifted flour to make a nice soft dough. Knead well and leave to rise in a warm place. When well risen, sift the remaining flour, salt and saffron and rub in the butter. Add the sugar, eggs and fermented dough. Knead well and work in the raisins. Put into two greased ½lb (200g) loaf tins (pans) and leave to rise. Bake in a moderately hot oven 375°F, 190°C, Gas Mark 5 for about 1¼ hours.

SAGE

(*Salvia officinalis*)

One of the old favourites, renowned for its healing properties. A hardy evergreen-grey shrub growing about 2 feet (65cm) high, with tough woody stems covered with 2 inch (5cm) long velvety leaves, oblong and pointed, and small pretty flowers of violet-blue forming in whorls at the tips of the stems.

The name salvia means to save or heal and it is reputed to cure all manner of alarming afflictions and disease, as well as to prolong life. There is a saying in many countries . . . 'How can a man die if he has sage in his garden?' Many country people take the precaution of chewing sage leaves and drinking sage tea daily.

One of the herbs which can do more good than harm to the body, but more harm than good to the incautious cook. Its powerful, spicy flavour can become bitter and violent if used to excess, but its main use is to counteract the richness of fat meats. The fresh, chopped leaves are essential in stuffings for goose, duck and pork and although the powdered and dried leaves are passable as a substitute in flavour, they have not the same powers in helping to digest fat.

Use sage in sausages, meat loaves and pies, in cheese, pea soup, pastry, wrapped round pieces of eel for the last part of cooking, and with grilled liver.

Cultivation
Sage will grow in any soil but prefers it to be well-drained and in full sun. The bushes are inclined to become 'leggy' but this can be controlled by clipping them back lightly when they have flowered . . . only the current year's growth, never into the old wood. They should be replaced in any case after three or four years, for as the wood hardens they produce fewer young leaves.

Propagation is easy from cuttings taken with a 'heel' in early summer and put in the open.

They make successful pot plants, kept well watered and clipped. The pots or containers must be large and in full sun.

Preserving
The leaves dry well but it is important to pick them in spring before any flower buds form, or the flavour may become musty. Hang the leaves in bunches in a warm, dry place, away

from strong sunlight. Leave until the leaves are quite dry—the length of time taken to dry them will depend on the temperature and atmosphere of the drying place. When quite dry crumble into airtight jars and label.

To freeze bunches of sage, pack into small polythene (plastic) bags and put straight into the freezer. These will keep well for up to two months. If wishing to store for a longer period blanch in boiling water, dip in cold water then dry well, pack and freeze.

Stuffings

Sage and Onion Stuffing

This quantity of stuffing is suitable for a 3lb (1·2 kilo) loin of pork or a 4lb (1·75 kilo) duck, but allow double the quantity for an 8lb (3·5 kilo) goose.

2 medium-sized onions
salt
3oz (75g/1 cup) fresh white breadcrumbs
1oz (25g/2 tablespoons) butter, melted
2 teaspoons chopped sage
freshly milled black pepper

Peel the onions and cook in a little boiling salted water for 30 minutes or until just tender. Drain thoroughly, then chop finely. Put into a basin with all the remaining ingredients and mix well. If the stuffing is a little dry, add a couple of teaspoons of the liquor from cooking the onions.

Fish

Eels with Bacon and Sage

This is an unusual combination, but the result is excellent.

2 medium-sized eels
3 tablespoons lemon juice
6 tablespoons olive oil
1 large onion, finely chopped
salt and freshly milled black pepper
1 teaspoon chopped parsley
1 teaspoon chopped dill
1 teaspoon chopped tarragon
12 rashers (slices) streaky (fat) bacon, de-rinded
12 large, or more smaller, sage leaves

Cut each eel into 6 pieces, and put into a shallow dish. Blend the lemon juice with the olive oil, onion, seasoning, parsley, dill and tarragon and pour over the eels. Leave to marinate for 2 hours, turning from time to time. Drain the pieces of eel and reserve the mar-

inade. Wrap each piece of eel, first in a rasher of bacon, then in 1 large or 2 smaller sage leaves. Tie with thread. Place in an ovenproof dish and strain over the remains of the marinade. Cook, uncovered, in a moderate oven, 350°F, 180°C, Gas Mark 4 for 30 minutes or until the eels are quite tender. (Serves 4—6)

Meat

Porker's Hotpot

1oz (25g/2 tablespoons) lard or dripping
12oz (300g) pork belly, thinly sliced
12oz (300g) pig's liver, thinly sliced
2 large onions, chopped
2 large carrots, chopped
2 sticks celery, chopped
1oz (25g/4 tablespoons) flour
¾ pint (375ml/2 cups) stock
1 tablespoon chopped sage
salt and pepper

Melt the lard or dripping in a large frying pan and fry the pork belly on both sides until golden. Remove from the pan with a slotted spoon and place in a casserole. Quickly fry the liver on each side for 2 minutes, then add to the pork. Fry the vegetables gently in the fat remaining for 10 minutes. Sprinkle over the flour and cook for a further 3 minutes, then gradually stir in the stock and bring to the boil, stirring all the time. Add the sage and seasoning and pour over the pork and liver. Stir gently, cover and cook in a moderate oven, 350°F, 180°C, Gas Mark 4 for 1½ hours. (Serves 4)

Saltimbocca

8 thin escalopes of veal about 2 oz (50g) each
8 thin slices lean ham
8 fresh sage leaves
salt and freshly milled black pepper
2oz (50g/¼ cup) butter
1 tablespoon olive oil
5 tablespoons dry white wine

Beat out the veal escalopes until they are about 4 inches x 5 inches (10cm x 12·5cm) or ask the butcher to do this for you. On each slice of meat, place a slice of ham and a sage leaf and season with salt and pepper. Turn in the sides of the meat and roll up. Secure with thread or cocktail sticks (toothpicks). Heat the butter and oil in a pan, add the veal rolls and cook until golden. Pour over the wine, cover and simmer gently for about 12 minutes or until the rolls are very tender. Remove the thread or sticks before serving. (Serves 4)

Poultry and Game

Chicken Breasts with Sage

3 large chicken breast joints
2 tablespoons flour
salt and pepper
1 tablespoon olive oil
½oz (15g/1 tablespoon) butter
4oz (100g) gammon rasher
¼ pint (125ml/⅝ cup) dry white wine
¼ pint (125ml/⅝ cup) stock
1 tablespoon chopped sage

Remove the skin of the chicken, cut off the wings and take the flesh off the bones. Cut the breasts in half lengthways. Toss in the flour, seasoned with salt and pepper. Heat the oil and butter in a pan, add the chicken and fry for about 5 minutes or until golden brown. Cut the gammon into thin strips and add to the chicken. Continue frying for a further 5 minutes, then add the wine, stock and sage. Bring to the boil, cover and simmer gently for 15 minutes. Remove the chicken and gammon to a heated serving dish using a slotted spoon. Boil the liquid in the sauce rapidly until it is reduced by about one-third then pour over the chicken. Serve at once. (Serves 6)

Hare in Madeira Sauce

1 hare, jointed
2oz (50g/½ cup) flour
salt and freshly milled black pepper
3 teaspoons chopped sage
4 tablespoons oil
4 rashers (slices) streaky (fat) bacon, de-rinded and chopped
½ pint (250ml/1¼ cups) Madeira
¼ pint (125ml/⅝ cup) stock
8oz (200g) button mushrooms
To Garnish:
1 tablespoon chopped parsley

Toss the hare in the flour seasoned with salt, pepper and the chopped sage. Heat the oil in a large frying pan and fry the bacon and hare until it is golden brown on all sides. Remove from the pan and place in a casserole. Sprinkle in any remaining flour and cook for a minute, then stir in the Madeira and stock and bring to the boil, stirring all the time. Pour over the joints of hare, cover and cook in a very moderate oven, 325°F, 170°C, Gas Mark 3 for 2½ hours. Add the mushrooms to the casserole 30 minutes before the end of cooking. Taste and adjust the seasoning and sprinkle with the parsley before serving. (Serves 6–8)

Pies and Flans

Sage and Leek Flan

For the Pastry:
6oz (150g/1½ cups) plain (all-purpose) flour
pinch salt
3oz (75g/⅜ cup) butter or margarine
about 1½ tablespoons water
For the Filling:
1lb (400g) leeks
1oz (25g/2 tablespoons) butter
1 tablespoon finely chopped sage
1 tablespoon chopped parsley
2 rashers (slices) streaky (fat) bacon, de-rinded and chopped
2 eggs, beaten
¼ pint (125ml/⅝ cup) single (light) cream or use milk
salt and pepper

Sift the flour and salt into a bowl. Cut the butter or margarine into pieces, and rub into the flour until the mixture resembles fine breadcrumbs. Bind with water to make a firm dough. Turn on to a floured surface, knead lightly, roll out and use the pastry to line an 8 inch (20cm) flan ring or tin. Fill the centre with greaseproof paper and baking beans and bake in a moderately hot oven, 400°F, 200°C, Gas Mark 6 for 15 minutes. Remove the greaseproof paper and beans and cook for a further 5 minutes to dry out the base. Reduce the oven temperature to 350°F, 180°C, Gas Mark 4.
Wash the leeks, thoroughly, then cut into slices. Melt the butter in a pan, add the leeks, cover and cook gently for about 15 minutes or until quite soft. Add all the remaining ingredients and mix well. Spoon into the flan case and cook for 30 minutes or until the custard is set and the top golden. (Serves 4–6)

SAVORY

(Satureja hortensi) Summer
(Satureja montana) Winter

There are two kinds, both highly peppery and spicy. Summer savory is an annual, about 12 inches (30cm) high and rather floppy. It has a lighter, more refined flavour than the easily grown winter type which is a perennial evergreen. This forms an attractive little bush, about 12 inches (30cm) high with small pointed leaves where pale mauve flowers later form at their base.

The fragrance of savory attracts a great gathering of bees, and if you have the ill luck to be stung, the pain is suposed to be relieved by rubbing savory leaves on the spot . . . if you can reach them without getting stung further!

Savory is the traditional companion for all bean dishes. Put sprigs into the boiling water and chop fresh leaves on to them when cooked, or into accompanying sauces. It is excellent in stews and salads, with pork and veal chops; chopped fresh on to tomato, potato, cucumber and bean salads, and on to mushrooms and tomatoes while they are being grilled.

Winter savory has the strongest, and to me, better flavour. Both should be used with caution so that they do not kill the taste of what they are intended only to enhance.

Cultivation
All savory likes to grow in the sun in well-drained soil. Sow the summer variety in the spring and thin seedlings to 6 inches (15cm). This will give you young leaves and shoots from mid-summer till frost cuts the plants down.

A regular supply throughout the winter can be enjoyed from pots grown indoors and kept on a sunny window-ledge.

Winter savory can put up with more spartan treatment than the annual kind, and can be picked from the garden throughout the year. The small bushes make useful path edgings in quite poor soil, or can be grown in a rock garden, in pots and window boxes. Although perennial, it is best to divide them every three or four years, discarding the hard centre and replanting the young outer roots. It can easily be propagated from cuttings taken in late spring; they root quickly in the open, in well-drained soil.

Preserving

There is little point in preserving Winter Savory as it is available all through the year. Summer however dries well. Pick the fresh young leaves in the morning after the dew has dried. Discard any brown or discoloured leaves. Hang the leaves in bunches in a warm, dry place, away from strong sunlight. Leave until the leaves are quite dry—the length of time taken to dry them will depend on the temperature and atmosphere of the drying place. When quite dry crumble into airtight jars and label.

Soups

Rich Onion Soup

2oz (50g/¼ cup) lard or dripping
1lb (400g) onions, peeled and finely chopped
1oz (25g/4 tablespoons) flour
1½ pints (750ml/3¾ cups) rich beef stock
1 tablespoon concentrated tomato purée
2 teaspoons chopped savory
salt and freshly milled black pepper

Melt the lard or dripping in a pan. Fry the onions gently for about 20 minutes or until they are just beginning to brown. Stir in the flour and cook over a very gentle heat for about 5 minutes or until a good golden brown. Gradually stir in the stock and bring to the boil, stirring all the time. Add the tomato purée, savory and seasoning. Cover and simmer gently for 30—40 minutes. Serve with crusty French bread. (Serves 6)

Hors d'œuvres

Prawn Cocktail with Savory

¼ pint (125ml/⅝ cup) natural yogurt
1½ tablespoons concentrated tomato purée
2 teaspoons chopped savory
½ teaspoon soy sauce
salt and pepper
6—8oz (150—200g) peeled prawns
To Garnish:
paprika

Tip the yogurt into a basin and add the tomato purée, savory, soy sauce and seasoning. Cover and put into the refrigerator for at least 1 hour before serving for the flavours to infuse. Just before serving, stir in the prawns, divide between 4 small bowls or glasses and sprinkle with paprika to garnish. (Serves 4)

Farmhouse Terrine

12oz (300g) streaky (fat) bacon rashers (slices)
12oz (300g) calf's liver
1 large onion
1½lb (600g) minced (ground) veal
2 cloves garlic, crushed
1 heaped tablespoon concentrated tomato purée
1 tablespoon chopped savory
2 teaspoons chopped oregano
4oz (100g/½ cup) softened butter
¼ pint (125ml/⅝ cup) red wine
salt and freshly milled black pepper
4 bay leaves

Cut off the rind from the bacon, lay it out on a board, then stretch with the back of a round-bladed knife. Use most of the rashers to line the bottom and sides of a terrine or ovenproof dish. Mince (grind) the liver and onion coarsely and put into a bowl with the veal, garlic, tomato purée, savory, oregano, butter and red wine. Mix well and season with salt and pepper. Spoon the mixture into the prepared terrine. Arrange the bay leaves on top and cover with the remaining bacon. Cover and stand in a roasting tin (pan) containing 1 inch (2.5cm) hot water. Cook in a moderate oven, 350°F, 180°C, Gas Mark 4 for 2½ hours. Remove the lid, lay a piece of foil on top and stand weights on this to press the terrine down as it cools. Leave for 2–3 days for the flavours to infuse before serving. (Serves 6–8)

Fish

Baked Fish with Cider

1½lb (600g) filleted white fish; cod, snapper, haddock, grouper
3 shallots, finely chopped
1 tablespoon chopped savory
2 apples, peeled, cored and diced
salt and pepper
generous ¼ pint (150ml/1 cup) cider
2oz (50g/¼ cup) butter
2oz (50g/⅔ cup) fresh white breadcrumbs

Lay the fillets in the bottom of a well buttered ovenproof dish. Cover with the shallots, savory, apples and seasoning. Pour over the cider. Melt the butter in a frying pan and fry the breadcrumbs until they are crisp and golden. Scatter over the top of the fish. Bake in a moderately hot oven, 375°F, 190°C, Gas Mark 5 for about 25 minutes or until the fish is tender and the top is golden. (Serves 4–6)

Meat

Roast Pork with Apple and Nut Stuffing

1oz (25g/2 tablespoons) butter
1 small onion, finely chopped
2oz (50g/½ cup) walnuts, chopped
2oz (50g) crustless white bread, diced
1 medium-sized cooking apple, peeled, cored and diced
1 stick celery, finely chopped
2 teaspoon chopped parsley
1½ tablespoons chopped savory
1 tablespoon lemon juice
salt and pepper
3lb (1·2 kilo) blade of pork, boned
2 tablespoons oil
¼ pint (125ml/⅝ cup) dry cider

Melt the butter and fry the onion and nuts for 5 minutes or until golden. Add the bread, apple and celery and continue cooking for about 5

minutes or until the apple is soft. Remove from the heat and add the parsley, savory, lemon juice and seasoning.
Lay the pork out flat on a board with the rind underneath. Open the pocket and spread the stuffing evenly, roll up and tie securely with string. Place the joint in a roasting tin (pan) and brush the rind with oil (this helps to make the crackling crisp) and season with salt. Roast in a moderately hot oven, 400°F, 200°C, Gas Mark 6 for 30 minutes, then lower the heat to 350°F, 180°C, Gas Mark 4 and cook for a further 1½ hours.
Place the joint on a heated serving dish and keep warm. Skim off all the fat from the pan juices. Add the cider and bring to the boil, scraping the bottom of the pan well. Season to taste and serve this gravy with the pork. (Serves 6–8)

Tripe with Savory

4 tablespoons oil
1 large onion, chopped
2 cloves garlic, crushed
2lb (800g) prepared tripe
2 tablespoons flour
salt and pepper
8oz (200g) mushrooms, sliced
1 tablespoon chopped savory
½ pint (250ml/1¼ cups) stock

Heat the oil in a fireproof casserole and fry the onion and garlic for 5 minutes. Cut the tripe into squares and toss in the flour, seasoned with salt and pepper. Add to the casserole and fry until golden. Add the mushrooms, savory and stock and stir well. Cover and cook in a very moderate oven, 325°F, 170°C, Gas Mark 3 for 1 hour. Taste and adjust the seasoning before serving. (Serves 6)

Variation: Add 4 large tomatoes, skinned, de-seeded and chopped, with the mushrooms.

Stuffed Peppers (Capsicums)

4 green peppers (capsicums)
salt
1 tablespoon olive oil
1 onion, chopped
8oz (200g) minced (ground) beef or pork
1 thick slice white bread
1 egg, beaten
salt and freshly milled black pepper
3 teaspoons chopped savory
1 tablespoon chopped parsley
2–3 tablespoons water

With a sharp knife, cut off the stalk end of the peppers (capsicums), remove the seeds but keep the tops intact. Put the peppers (capsicums) into a pan of boiling salted water for 2–3 minutes, then drain in a colander, and stand upside down for all the water to drain off while preparing the stuffing. Heat the oil in a pan and fry the onion for 5 minutes. Add the meat and cook, stirring frequently until the meat has browned. Remove from the heat. Cut the crusts off the bread, lay on a plate and pour over the egg. Leave to soak for 2–3 minutes, then mash and add to the meat with the seasoning, savory and parsley. Spoon the stuffing into the peppers (capsicums) and replace the lids. Stand the peppers (capsicums) close together in an ovenproof dish; if they will not stand upright, cut a small piece off the bottom of each one. Pour over the water. Cover and bake in a moderately hot oven, 375°F, 190°C, Gas Mark 5 for 30 minutes. Serve the peppers (capsicums) with a fresh tomato sauce (see page 20). (Serves 4)

Family Meat Loaf

1lb (400g) lean minced (ground) beef
8oz (200g) good quality pork sausagemeat
2oz (50g/⅔ cup) fresh white breadcrumbs
1 onion, grated
1 tablespoon chopped parsley
2 teaspoons chopped chives
2 teaspoons chopped savory
2 teaspoons Worcestershire sauce
salt and freshly milled black pepper
2 eggs, beaten

Mix all the ingredients together and bind with the beaten eggs. Turn into a well-greased 2lb (800g) loaf tin (pan) and cover with foil. Stand in a roasting tin (pan) containing 1 inch (2·5cm) of cold water and bake in a moderate oven, 350°F, 180°C, Gas Mark 4 for 1½ hours. If serving cold, put a weight on top of the loaf while it is cooling. (Serves 6)

Poultry

Normandy Duck

This dish looks very attractive garnished with slices of red-skinned apple.

4lb (1·75 kilo) duck
1oz (25g/2 tablespoons) butter
1 onion, chopped
1oz (25g/4 tablespoons) flour
¼ pint (125ml/⅝ cup) stock made from the giblets of the duck
¼ pint (125ml/⅝ cup) dry cider
1 tablespoon chopped savory
salt and pepper
2 dessert apples, peeled, cored and sliced
3 tablespoons double (heavy) cream

Place the duck in a roasting tin (pan). Melt the butter in a small pan, add the onion and cook gently for 5 minutes. Stir in the flour and cook until golden, then gradually stir in the stock and cider. Add the savory, seasoning and apples and pour over the duck. Cover with foil and roast in a hot oven, 425°F, 220°C, Gas Mark 7 for 45 minutes, basting once or twice during cooking. Remove the foil and roast for a further 20 minutes or until the duck is tender. Remove the duck from the pan, carve it, place on a heated serving dish and keep warm. Skim off the excess fat from the pan juices, stir in the cream and heat gently without boiling. Taste and adjust the seasoning then pour over the duck. (Serves 3–4)

Vegetables and Salads

Savory with Beans

Savory has a remarkable effect on all beans by making them taste more bean-like while sacrificing its own individual flavour. Put a sprig of savory in the water when cooking any type of beans—French, broad or runner. Strain the beans and remove this, then either serve the beans with a white sauce to which chopped savory has been added, or toss in melted butter mixed with chopped savory and freshly milled black pepper.

Beans with Ham

3lb (1·2 kilo) broad beans
salt
¼ pint (125ml/⅝ cup) single (light) cream
1 tablespoon chopped savory
6oz (150g) cooked ham or gammon, chopped
freshly milled black pepper

Shell the beans and cook in boiling salted water for about 10 minutes, drain well. Return to the pan and add the cream, savory, ham or gammon and plenty of seasoning. Heat gently, without allowing the mixture to boil. Taste and adjust the seasoning. (Serves 3–4)

SORREL

(*Rumex scutatus*) French

Sorrels are rather like docks, with astringent, fleshy, pointed leaves shaped as an arrowhead. There are various kinds, including wild sorrel, which has smaller leaves and a more bitter taste than the cultivated ones. It is a herbaceous perennial, and one of the few herbs to like a rich moist soil and partial shade.

Sorrel can be spiteful to the taste when wrongly cooked or used. But if it is a case of grinning and bearing it, there are many solaces . . . good for the blood, kidneys and digestion as well as a stimulant for the appetite.

It is renowned as a piquant soup in many parts of Europe. The young leaves are most obliging 'mixers' both raw and cooked in salads and as a vegetable purée or sauce. The slightly tart flavour flows into and enhances spinach, lettuce and cabbage. The fresh young leaves make a remarkable difference to omelettes or scrambled eggs, scissored in at the last moment, or used whole and crisp in any sandwich which needs smartening up with a touch of lemon.

Sorrel leaves torn up in a mixed salad are specially good with fish dishes and cold meats. Whole large leaves wrapped round a joint of meat act as a tenderiser as well as flavouring . . . try it round veal, pork and whole baked fish.

Cultivation

Sorrel is easy to grow from seed sown in spring or autumn, but will take over a year to produce enough leaves for even a sandwich. Beg or buy roots and set them in clumps about 12 inches (30cm) apart in autumn or early spring. The plants grow from 12–18 inches (30–45cm) and any flower buds must be removed. They must be picked hard and constantly, to keep them in full flush. They retreat in a severe winter but the brave young leaves reappear as soon as they dare. To keep the roots healthy and productive, dig them up every four years, divide them and replant the best parts.

Preserving

The leaves can be picked at any time the plant is most robust, and dried flat in an airy shady place, then crumbled into airtight jars. It is much better though to pot up a few roots before the frost and keep them in the house, or put a cloche over some of the plants in the open garden, to keep up a supply of fresh leaves. The frozen leaves are not satisfactory for salads, but sorrel purée can be frozen successfully, and used as in the recipes below.

109

Soups

Cream of Sorrel Soup

This soup can either be served hot or chilled with one or two ice cubes floating in each bowl.

8oz (200g) sorrel leaves
8oz (200g) spinach
salt
1½oz (40g) butter
1 small onion, finely chopped
1½oz (40g/6 tablespoons) flour
1 pint (500ml/2½ cups) milk
¾ pint (375ml/2 cups) chicken stock
salt and freshly milled black pepper
¼ pint (125ml/⅝ cup) single (light) cream
1 egg yolk
about 1 tablespoon lemon juice
pinch sugar

Wash the leaves thoroughly. Cook the sorrel and spinach in separate pans in a little boiling salted water until tender, about 10 minutes. Drain well and either sieve or purée in a blender. Melt the butter in a pan and fry the onion gently for 5 minutes. Stir in the flour and cook for a minute, then gradually stir in the milk and stock and bring to the boil, stirring all the time. Add the spinach and sorrel purées and seasoning and beat well, then stir in the cream, blended with the egg yolk, lemon juice and sugar. Do not allow the soup to boil after the cream has been added. Taste and adjust the seasoning. Serve either hot or cold. (Serves 4–6)

Iced Spring Soup

2oz (50g) sorrel leaves
1 small lettuce or the outside leaves of a
   large lettuce
1 bunch watercress
1½oz (40g/3 tablespoons) butter
¾ pint (375ml/2 cups) chicken stock
2 egg yolks
½ pint (250ml/1¼ cups) soured cream
salt and pepper
1 tablespoon chopped chives

Wash the sorrel, lettuce and watercress. Trim off about half the watercress stalks. Melt the butter in a pan, add the leaves, cover and cook until they are tender, about 10–15 minutes. Sieve or put into a blender until smooth. Replace the purée in the saucepan with the chicken stock and bring to the boil. Beat the egg

yolks with 2 tablespoons of the cream. Pour on about 4 tablespoons of the hot stock, stir well then tip back into the pan. Heat gently, without boiling until the mixture thickens. Remove from the heat and when cold, stir in the remaining soured cream and season to taste. Chill well and sprinkle with chives before serving. (Serves 4–6)

Lentil and Sorrel Soup

4oz (100g/½ cup) green or brown lentils
2½ pints (1·25 litres/6¼ cups) water
1 onion, finely chopped
salt and pepper
4oz (100g) sorrel leaves
1oz (25g/2 tablespoons) butter
stock (see method)
2 tablespoons double (heavy) cream

Put the lentils into a pan with the water and onion. Cover, bring to the boil and cook for about 1½ hours or until the lentils are quite tender. Add salt towards the end of cooking. Wash the sorrel. Melt the butter in a small pan, add the sorrel, cover and cook until it is tender, about 5–10 minutes. Add to the lentils, then either put the soup through a sieve or vegetable mouli or put into a blender to make a smooth purée. If the soup is too thick, add a little stock. Reheat the soup, stir in the cream and taste and adjust the seasoning. (Serves 4–6)

Fish

Stuffed Mackerel with Sorrel

4 medium-sized mackerel, about 12oz
   (300g) each
3oz (75g/⅜ cup) butter
2oz (50g/⅔ cup) fresh, white breadcrumbs
4 tablespoons chopped sorrel
salt and pepper
2 tablespoons lemon juice

Cut off the heads from the mackerel, clean and bone them. Lay them out flat on a board with the skin side down. Melt 2oz (50g/¼ cup) of the butter and blend with the breadcrumbs, sorrel and seasoning. Divide this stuffing between the fish, then roll them up, starting at the head end. Place fairly close together in an ovenproof dish, dot with the remaining butter, lightly season and pour over the lemon juice. Cover and bake in a moderately hot oven, 400°F, 200°C, Gas Mark 6 for 30–35 minutes. (Serves 4)

Mackerel Baked with Sorrel

4 medium-sized mackerel
2 tablespoons olive oil
salt and freshly milled black pepper
large sorrel leaves (see method)

Clean the fish, brush all over with oil and season with salt and pepper. Wrap each fish completely in large sorrel leaves and place in an ovenproof dish. Cover and bake in a moderately hot oven, 375°F, 190°C, Gas Mark 5 for about 25 minutes or until the fish are cooked. Discard the sorrel leaves before serving. (Serves 4)

Meat

Roast Veal with Sorrel

2oz (50g/¼ cup) butter
2 cloves garlic, crushed
salt and freshly milled black pepper
grated zest of ½ lemon
3lb (1·2 kilo) boned breast or leg of veal
large sorrel leaves (see method)

Cream the butter and beat in the garlic, seasoning and lemon zest. Rub this all over the joint. Completely cover the joint with large sorrel leaves and tie into place with string. Put into a roasting tin (pan) and roast in a moderate oven, 350°F, 180°C, Gas Mark 4 for 2 hours, basting from time to time. If you wish to brown the meat, remove the leaves 30 minutes before the end of cooking time, otherwise remove before serving. (Serves 6–8)

Eggs and Cheese

Green Eggs

3oz (75g) sorrel leaves
1oz (25g/2 tablespoons) butter
salt and pepper
8 hard-boiled eggs
1½oz (40g/3 tablespoons) cream cheese
2 tablespoons grated Wensleydale or
    Cheddar cheese
pinch grated nutmeg

Wash the sorrel leaves. Melt the butter in a pan, add the sorrel leaves and seasoning. Cover and cook gently until the leaves are very tender, about 10 minutes. Drain and chop the leaves finely, sieve or put into a blender. Halve the eggs, scoop out the yolks and sieve them. Beat together the sorrel purée, egg yolks and cheeses and season with salt, pepper and nutmeg. Pile this mixture back into the egg whites and serve on a bed of watercress with a French dressing. (Serves 4–6)

Sorrel Soufflé

1oz (25g/2 tablespoons) butter
1oz (25g/4 tablespoons) flour
generous ¼ pint (150ml/1 cup) milk
2oz (50g/½ cup) Gruyère (Swiss) cheese,
    grated
5 tablespoons sorrel purée (see below)
good pinch grated nutmeg
salt and freshly milled black pepper
½ teaspoon French mustard
4 eggs, separated

Melt the butter in a pan, add the flour and cook for 1 minute. Gradually stir in the milk and bring to the boil, stirring all the time. Remove from the heat and beat in the cheese, sorrel purée, nutmeg, seasoning, mustard and egg yolks. Whisk the egg whites until they form stiff peaks then fold into the sorrel mixture. Turn into a 2½ pint (1·25 litre/6¼ cup) soufflé dish and bake in a moderately hot oven, 375°F, 190°C, Gas Mark 5 for about 30 minutes or until well risen and golden brown. (Serves 3–4)

Vegetables and Salads

Sorrel Purée

This purée can be used in the same way as spinach purée, but in particular makes a delicious filling for omelettes.

1lb (400g) sorrel
salt
½oz (15g/1 tablespoon) butter
¼ pint (125ml/⅝ cup) single (light) cream
2 egg yolks
1 tablespoon chopped parsley
freshly milled black pepper

Wash the sorrel well and cook in a very little boiling salted water until tender, about 5–10 minutes. Drain well and either chop finely, sieve or put into a blender.
Melt the butter in a pan, add the sorrel purée and heat gently, then stir in the cream, blended with the egg yolks, parsley and seasoning. Heat gently without allowing the purée to boil. (Serves 4)

Dandelion and Sorrel Salad

To grow dandelions for use in salads, it is best to cover the plants with a large flowerpot to keep off the light, otherwise the leaves tend to be rather tough and bitter.

8oz (200g) dandelion leaves
4oz (100g) sorrel leaves
3 tablespoons oil
1½ tablespoons lemon juice
pinch sugar
salt and freshly milled black pepper

Wash and dry the dandelion and sorrel leaves. Put into a polythene bag and leave to crisp for 1 hour in the refrigerator, then turn into a salad bowl. Put all the remaining ingredients into a screw-topped jar and shake well to mix. Pour over the salad and toss lightly before serving. (Serves 4)

Potato Salad with Sorrel

1½lb (600g) potatoes
salt
1 medium-sized onion, finely chopped
1 dessert apple, cored and chopped
2 tablespoons lemon juice
1 tablespoon chopped lovage
4 tablespoons oil
freshly milled black pepper
4oz (100g) sorrel leaves

Peel the potatoes and cook in boiling salted water until tender. Drain and dice them and put into a bowl. Add the onion, the apple, tossed with the lemon juice, lovage, oil and seasoning and toss well together. Leave to cool. Wash and dry the sorrel leaves and line a salad bowl with them, then spoon the cold potato mixture into the centre. (Serves 4)

Prawn and Sorrel Salad

2oz (50g) sorrel leaves
1 lettuce heart
8oz (200g) peeled prawns
4 tablespoons olive oil
2 tablespoons lemon juice
pinch dry mustard
salt and freshly milled black pepper
pinch sugar
1 tablespoon chopped chives

Wash and dry the sorrel and lettuce and tear the leaves into small pieces. Put into a salad bowl with the prawns. Put all the remaining ingredients into a screw-topped jar and shake well. Pour over the salad and toss together just before serving. (Serves 3–4)

Variation: Use cooked white fish in place of the prawns or use half white fish and half prawns.

Breads

Double Decker Sandwich

2 slices white bread
1 slice brown bread
½oz (15g/1 tablespoon) butter
1 tablespoon mayonnaise
1 teaspoon finely chopped celery
1 teaspoon concentrated tomato purée
salt and freshly milled black pepper
1 tablespoon peeled prawns
4 sorrel leaves (washed and dried)
1 large tomato, sliced

Butter the slices of white bread on one side and the slice of brown bread on both sides. Blend the mayonnaise, celery, tomato purée and seasoning together. Stir in the prawns. Spread this over one slice of white bread and top with the slice of brown bread. Arrange the sorrel leaves and tomato slices on the brown bread and cover with the remaining slice of white bread. Remove the crusts if wished and cut into triangles before serving. (Serves 1)

Variations: Use small shrimps or cooked crab-meat in place of the prawns. Use slices of cucumber instead of, or as well as, the tomato. Put the sorrel leaves onto a piece of buttered French bread, lay the tomato slices on top. Spoon over the prawn mixture and top with another piece of French bread.

114

TARRAGON

(Artemisia dracunculus)

French tarragon, which has justifiably been described as the king of all culinary herbs, has a distinctive flavour quite unlike any other. A moderately hardy perennial, it grows to about 2½ feet (85cm) with slender, stiffly elegant stems, branching out and covered in small, tender, narrow, green leaves, up to 3 inches (7·5cm) long. When squeezed, they give off a sweetly pungent scent, slightly peppery.

Tarragon is essential for any respectable cooking. The individual aroma of French tarragon is at its most perfect with certain foods when used as the only flavouring; in particular as a sauce served with boiled chicken . . . a world renowned combination. Its other close affinity is with fish, as either a stuffing or sauce. Use the young tender leaves chopped in soups, salads, butters, mayonnaise, sauce Bearnaise, on potatoes, mushrooms, seafood, liver, kidney and game. Use whole sprigs inside roast chicken with nothing more than a large lump of butter and a clove of chopped or crushed garlic.

Cultivation

True French tarragon does not grow from seed, you have to start with cuttings or root divisions. Have a care when buying. The only seed available to the general public is usually Russian tarragon (*Artemisia dracunculoides*), which is a waste of space and temper. It grows vigorously up to 6 feet (2 metres), and what little flavour it has is unpleasant. There is no decorative value either and if you accidentally find yourself growing it, the only remedy is to dig out every bit of root and burn it, unless your particular soil does something remarkable to transform the aroma.

French tarragon could not be described as robust, but once you find the place it likes most, it will thrive and demand to be split up year after year, so that you are never without.

The plants like to grow in full sun in very well-drained soil . . . This does not mean

however, that they can be starved. Put plenty of well-decayed humus into the ground before planting, which will keep it moist but not boggy, during the growing period. Side pieces of root can be taken off in spring and replanted, but the whole parent plant should be dug up and replanted in fresh soil every four years in early spring. Take care in teasing apart the closely entangled roots.

Tarragon can be grown in pots and containers if they are large enough for the roots to grow freely. They will need splitting or repotting every two or three years. When this is necessary never lose your temper disentangling the roots, by cutting or twisting. They must be patiently unravelled . . . in a bucket of water if necessary.

The leaves wither away in winter, but don't be tempted to cut down the brittle stems till new shoots spring from the ground early in the year. Only really severe cold and frost will kill the plants while they are resting in winter; they need some protection in hard climates.

Preserving

The leaves dry well if whole shoots are taken early in the year, though lose all but a whiff of their unique aroma. Pick the fresh young leaves in the morning after the dew has dried. Discard any brown or discoloured leaves. Hang the leaves in bunches in a warm dry place, away from strong sunlight, an airing cupboard would be ideal. Leave until the leaves are quite dry—the length of time taken to dry the leaves will depend on the temperature and atmosphere of the drying place. When quite dry crumble into airtight jars.

To freeze, pack small bunches in polythene bags straight into the freezer where they will keep well for up to two months. If you want to keep the herb for a longer period, blanch in boiling water for 1 minute, drain, dip in cold water, dry well, pack into polythene bags and freeze.

Alternatively, chop the leaves and pack lightly into an ice cube tray. Top up with water and freeze. When frozen, turn out into polythene bags and store in the freezer. Take out cubes as required, defrost in a strainer and use as fresh.

Soups

Tomato, Orange and Tarragon Soup

2 tablespoons oil
1 medium-sized onion, chopped
1 medium-sized potato, peeled and sliced
1½lb (600g) ripe tomatoes, skinned and chopped
2 teaspoons chopped tarragon
1 clove garlic, crushed
½ pint (250ml/1¼ cups) stock
salt and freshly milled black pepper
juice of ½ orange
1 teaspoon grated orange zest
pinch sugar (see method)

Heat the oil in a pan and gently fry the onion and potato for 5 minutes. Add the tomatoes, tarragon and garlic, blend well then stir in the stock and seasoning. Cover and simmer gently for 20 minutes. Either put into a liquidizer and blend for a minute or rub through a sieve or vegetable mouli, then blend with the strained liquid. Stir in the orange juice and zest, then taste and adjust the seasoning, adding sugar if necessary. Chill well before serving. (Serves 4–6)

Tarragon Soup

This is a very light, clear soup. For a thicker soup add 2 egg yolks, beaten with ¼ pint (125ml/⅝ cup) single (light) cream and heat gently without boiling.

1 pint (500ml/2½ cups) chicken or fish stock
2 teaspoons chopped tarragon
1 tablespoon grated Parmesan cheese
salt and pepper

Heat the stock with the tarragon and simmer gently for 2–3 minutes. Just before serving, stir in the cheese and taste and adjust the season-ing. (Serves 3–4)

Sauces

Tarragon mayonnaise

This sauce goes well with cold salmon or salmon trout, or other cold fish.

4 sprigs parsley
3 sprigs tarragon
3 sprigs chervil
small bunch spinach (about 2oz/50g)
salt
½ pint (250ml/1¼ cups) mayonnaise
2 tablespoons double (heavy) cream
freshly milled black pepper

Cook the parsley, tarragon, chervil and spinach in a very little boiling salted water until just tender, about 8 minutes. Drain well and either sieve or put into a blender. Shortly before serving, add this purée to the mayonnaise with the cream and season to taste; if you add the purée to the mayonnaise too early it will lose its colour. (Serves 4–6)

Rémoulade Sauce

This can be served with grilled (broiled) meat or fish.

½ pint (250ml/1¼ cups) mayonnaise
2 teaspoons French mustard
2 teaspoons capers, finely chopped
1 teaspoon chopped parsley
1 teaspoon chopped tarragon
1 teaspoon chopped chervil

Put the mayonnaise into a bowl, add all the remaining ingredients and mix well. Allow the sauce to stand for at least 30 minutes before serving for the flavours to infuse. (Serves 4)

Béarnaise Sauce

There are several different ways of making this sauce, but this is a fairly simple and straightforward recipe.

4 tablespoons white wine vinegar
6 peppercorns
½ bay leaf
1 sprig tarragon
1 sprig chervil (optional)
1 small shallot, finely chopped
3 egg yolks
4oz (100g/½ cup) softened butter
salt
2 teaspoons chopped tarragon
pepper

Put the vinegar, peppercorns, bay leaf, tarragon, chervil, if using, and shallot into a small pan. Bring to the boil and boil rapidly until it is reduced to about 1 tablespoon. Put the egg yolks, a nut of butter and pinch of salt into a basin over a pan of hot, *not boiling* water. Beat well with a whisk, then strain in the vinegar and mix well. Gradually add the butter to the mixture a dessertspoonful at a time, whisking well. When all the butter has been incorporated the mixture should be thick and glossy. Add the chopped tarragon and taste and adjust the seasoning before serving. (Serves 4)

Tarragon Cream Sauce for Fish

3oz (75g/⅜ cup) butter
¼ pint (125ml/⅝ cup) double (heavy) cream
1 tablespoon chopped tarragon (or more if you prefer)
1 tablespoon lemon juice
salt and pepper

Put the butter into a small pan over a gentle heat and as soon as it has melted, stir in the cream. Simmer until the cream is thick, then add the tarragon, lemon juice and seasoning and heat gently for 2–3 minutes. (Serves 4)

Gooseberry Sauce

Serve with mackerel, herrings or other oily fish.

½ pint (250ml/1¼ cups) water
8oz (200g) gooseberries
2 tablespoons sugar
1½oz (40g/3 tablespoons) butter
1 tablespoon flour
salt and freshly milled black pepper
2 teaspoons chopped tarragon

Bring half the water to the boil in a small saucepan. Add the gooseberries and simmer for 20 minutes or until the gooseberries are soft. Remove from the heat and sieve into a bowl, discarding the pips. Add the sugar to the purée. Melt 1 tablespoon of the butter, add the flour and cook for a minute. Gradually stir in the remaining water and bring to the boil, stirring well. Reduce the heat and stir in the gooseberry purée. Gradually add the remaining butter to the pan in small pieces. Season to taste and stir in the tarragon. (Serves 4)

Hors d'œuvres

Avocado Pears with Shellfish

If you wish to prepare this dish in advance, brush the cut surfaces of the avocado pear with lemon juice to prevent them from discolouring, but it should not be prepared more than about 1 hour before serving.

2 large avocado pears
6oz (150g) peeled prawns or lobster or crab meat
6 tablespoons cold Tarragon Cream Sauce (see above)
1 tablespoon chopped parsley

Cut the avocado pears in half and remove the stones. Blend the prawns or lobster or crab meat with the sauce and pile into the centres of the avocado pears. Sprinkle with parsley before serving. (Serves 4)

Pears in Tarragon Cream

This is a very simple and refreshing hors d'oeuvre.

6 firm, but ripe, dessert pears
2 tablespoons tarragon vinegar
½ pint (250ml/1¼ cups) double (heavy) cream
pinch sugar
salt and freshly milled black pepper
2 teaspoons chopped tarragon

Peel the pears, cut them in half and scoop out the cores with a teaspoon. Brush them with a very little tarragon vinegar to prevent them from browning and place in a circle on a serving plate, with the cut sides downwards. Lightly whip the cream with the vinegar until thick, but it should not be too stiff. Season with a little sugar and salt and pepper and spoon over the pears. Sprinkle with the chopped tarragon and chill in the refrigerator for 30 minutes before serving. (Serves 6)

Poultry

Tarragon Chicken

3oz (75g/⅜ cup) butter
2 tablespoons chopped tarragon
salt and freshly milled black pepper
3lb (1·2 kilo) roasting chicken
1 onion, sliced
2 teaspoons flour
¼ pint (125ml/⅝ cup) double (heavy) cream

Cream all but 2 teaspoons of the butter with 1 tablespoon of the tarragon and season with salt and pepper. Use two-thirds of this mixture to stuff inside the chicken and spread the remainder over the chicken. Put into a fireproof casserole or roasting tin (pan) and add the onion. Roast in a moderately hot oven, 375°F, 190°C, Gas Mark 5 for 1½ hours. Remove the chicken, place on a heated serving dish and keep warm. Blend the remaining butter with the flour, and gradually add to the juices in the casserole or tin (pan). Add the cream, heat gently without boiling, then stir in the remaining tarragon and season to taste. Serve the sauce with the chicken. (Serves 4-6)

Eggs and Cheese

Hard-boiled Eggs with Tarragon

Shell and quarter 6 hard-boiled eggs and add to the Tarragon Cream Sauce, above. Heat gently for 5 minutes. Serve sprinkled with 1—2 teaspoons chopped tarragon.

Poached Eggs with Tarragon

1 tablespoon chopped tarragon
½ pint (250ml/1¼ cups) béchamel sauce (page 26)
8 eggs
8 slices buttered toast

Add the tarragon to the sauce and simmer gently for 2—3 minutes. Poach the eggs and drain them well. Place on the buttered toast and pour over the sauce just before serving. (Serves 4)

Scrambled Eggs and Omelettes

Add chopped tarragon to an omelette just before you fold it over—allow 1—2 teaspoons for a 2 egg omelette. Sprinkle over scrambled eggs just before serving.

Preserves

Tarragon Vinegar

Put one or two sprigs of tarragon into a bottle. Pour over enough wine vinegar to completely fill the bottle, then cover, preferably with a cork and leave for at least 2 weeks before using.

THYME

Common thyme
(*Thymus vulgaris*)

Lemon thyme
(*Thymus citriodorus*)

There are many thymes, for many purposes from making lawns to stuffing pillows. These are the two most valuable in cooking. They are shrubby, decorative little evergreens, growing to about 12 inches (30cm) high and familiar on stony coasts and mountains of Mediterranean countries. Invaluable and easy to accommodate in any garden; the bees make particularly merry with the spikes of lilac flowers.

Common thyme is mostly used in casseroles and stuffings, and is a most important ingredient of a bouquet garni. Lemon thyme is less dominating and imparts a fruity flavour, which is strangely in harmony with meat balls, as well as baked custard!

Shred the tiny leaves from their stems and use fresh or dried in any stuffings for poultry or veal; in soups, salads, stews, meat loaves, fish dishes; and sprinkled on to vegetables such as aubergines (eggplants), onions, beetroot (beets), carrots and tomatoes. For sauces thyme is added during the cooking . . . always sparingly, or what should be a subtle undertone, can become overwhelming.

Cultivation

Thyme thrives in any very well-drained sunny soil particularly on a stony slope. Their only failing is a tendency to straggle, but this can be checked by snipping off the flowers as

soon as they have faded. Lemon thyme does not seed and new young plants have to be bought every three years. Or you can keep up a supply by pegging down low-growing branches of the old plants into the surrounding soil, and once rooted, cut them free and transplant.

Common thyme is easily grown from seed and will usually provide a large scattering of self-sown seedlings if you are not too diligent about removing the faded flower heads.

Both kinds make excellent inhabitants of window boxes and pots, in full sun and sandy soil and kept well fed.

Preserving

The dried leaves are much more aromatic than the fresh ones. Cut sprigs before the plant flowers. Hang in a dry shady place for a few weeks, then rub the leaves from the brittle stems and store in airtight jars.

To freeze, pack small bunches in polythene bags straight into the freezer and store for up to 2 months, or if you want to keep the herb for a longer period, blanch them in boiling water for 1 minute, drain, dip in cold water, dry well, pack into polythene bags and freeze.

Stuffings

Sausagemeat and Celery Stuffing

This quantity will stuff the vent end of a 12lb (5 kilo) dressed turkey, so use half the quantity for an average roasting chicken of 3–4lb (1·2–1·75 kilo) for stuffing both the neck and the vent end.

1lb (400g) good quality pork sausagemeat
1 onion, finely chopped
2 sticks celery, finely chopped

2 tablespoons chopped parsley
1 tablespoon chopped thyme
8oz (200g/2⅔ cups) fresh white
    breadcrumbs
salt and pepper
grated zest and juice 1 lemon
2 eggs, beaten

Combine all the ingredients and mix well to blend them.

Soups

Parsnip and Tomato Soup

1oz (25g/2 tablespoons) butter
2 onions, chopped
1 clove garlic, crushed
1lb (400g) parsnips, peeled and chopped
3 tablespoons flour
salt and pepper
1½ teaspoons chopped thyme
1½ pints (750ml/3¾ cups) chicken stock
¼ pint (125ml/⅝ cup) milk
1 bay leaf
12oz (300g) tomatoes, chopped

Melt the butter, add the onions and fry for 5 minutes. Add the garlic and parsnips and fry for a further 5 minutes. Stir in the flour, seasoning and thyme, then gradually stir in the stock, milk, bay leaf and tomatoes. Bring to the boil, stirring all the time. Cover and simmer gently for 40 minutes. Remove the bay leaf and either put the vegetables through a sieve or vegetable mouli and blend with the strained stock or put into a blender to make a smooth purée. Return to the pan and heat gently for 3–4 minutes before serving. (Serves 4–6)

Tomato, Carrot and Thyme Soup

8oz (200g) carrots, grated
12oz (300g) tomatoes, skinned and chopped
4 shallots, chopped
1 clove garlic, crushed
2 teaspoons paprika
2 teaspoons lemon juice
1 large bunch of thyme, tied with a piece of thread
3 pints (1·5 litres/7½ cups) chickens stock
salt and pepper
1½ tablespoons chopped parsley, chervil, or chives

Put all the ingredients, except the parsley, chervil or chives into a saucepan. Cover and simmer for 30 minutes. Remove the thyme, taste and adjust the seasoning. Serve sprinkled with the parsley, chervil or chives. (Serves 6)

Hors d'œuvres

Rillettes de Porc

4lb (1·75 kilo) lean pork belly
3 sprigs thyme
1 bay leaf

2 cloves garlic
salt and freshly milled black pepper
4 tablespoons water

Remove the skin and all the bones from the pork and cut into ½ inch (1·25 cm) cubes. Put into an ovenproof dish with the thyme, bay leaf, garlic, seasoning and water. Cover and cook in a slow oven, 300°F, 150°C, Gas Mark 1 for 3 hours.

Place a sieve over a bowl and turn the pork mixture into the sieve. Discard any large pieces of pork fat then roughly mash the meat, a little at a time, on a board with two forks. Pack the pork firmly into a dish, then pour the strained juices and fat over the top. The pork fat will form a complete seal over the meat which can be stored in a refrigerator for several weeks. (Serves 8)

Zeilook
(Moroccan Vegetable Purée)

¼ pint (125ml/⅝ cup) olive oil
1 onion, chopped
2 aubergines (eggplants), sliced
2 courgettes (zucchini), sliced
2 large tomatoes, skinned and sliced
2 teaspoons chopped thyme
good pinch cayenne pepper
salt
To Garnish:
green olives

Heat the oil in a pan and fry the onion for 5 minutes. Add the aubergines (eggplants) and courgettes (zucchini), cover and cook gently for 10 minutes. Add the remaining ingredients and simmer for about 20 minutes in a covered pan.

Mash the mixture with a vegetable masher to break it down. Cook at a high temperature in an open pan for about 5 minutes, stirring frequently until the mixture thickens. Remove from the heat, mash again and cook the mixture for a further 5 minutes, stirring all the time. Remove from the heat, taste and adjust the seasoning. Turn into a serving dish, allow to cool and chill for at least 3 hours before serving. Garnish with olives. (Serves 4–6)

Meat

Roasts

Rub chopped thyme into joints of beef and veal before roasting or over the skin of chicken and other poultry. A sprig or two of thyme can also be placed inside a bird during roasting.

Grills (Broils)

Chopped thyme is excellent sprinkled on steaks before they are grilled (broiled), or marinate a piece of steak in a mixture of oil and wine vinegar with chopped thyme and seasoning for 2–3 hours before cooking. This will help to tenderise the steak, as well as giving a good flavour. Chicken is also improved if it is sprinkled with thyme before grilling (broiling). Put a sprig of thyme inside mackerel, herring or trout before grilling (broiling) and remove before serving.

Beef Carbonnade

1½lb (600g) stewing steak
1oz (25g/2 tablespoons) lard or dripping
2 large onions, chopped
1oz (25g/4 tablespoons) flour
½ pint (250ml/1¼ cups) light ale
¼ pint (125ml/⅝ cup) water
1 tablespoon chopped thyme
1 teaspoon sugar
salt and pepper

Cut the beef into 1½ inch (3·75cm) cubes. Heat the lard or dripping in a pan and brown the meat quickly on all sides. Remove from the pan with a slotted spoon and put on one side. Add the onions to the pan and fry for 10 minutes or until golden. Blend in the flour and cook for 1 minute. Gradually stir in the ale and water, bring to the boil, stirring all the time and allow to thicken. Replace the meat in the pan with the remaining ingredients. Cover and simmer gently for 2 hours. Taste and adjust the seasoning before serving. (Serves 4)

Spanish Fried Liver and Thyme

1lb (400g) sliced lamb's or calf's liver
2 tablespoons flour
salt and pepper
2 teaspoons chopped thyme
2 tablespoons oil
1oz (25g/2 tablespoons) butter
juice of 1 large orange
2 tablespoons chopped parsley

Toss the liver slices in the flour, seasoned with salt, pepper and thyme. Heat the oil and butter in a frying pan and fry the liver gently for about 8 minutes, turning once. Remove from the pan and place on a heated serving dish and keep warm. Add the orange juice to the juices in the pan, simmer gently for 2–3 minutes, then pour over the liver and serve, sprinkled with the parsley. (Serves 4)

Poultry

French Rabbit Casserole

4–6 rabbit pieces
salt and pepper
1oz (25g/2 tablespoons) butter
4 rashers (slices) streaky (fat) bacon, de-rinded and chopped
1lb (400g) button onions, peeled
1 clove garlic, crushed
1oz (25g/4 tablespoons) flour
¼ pint (125ml/⅝ cup) water
½ pint (250ml/1¼ cups) red wine
2 teaspoons French mustard
4oz (100g) mushrooms
3 sprigs thyme

Wash the rabbit joints and dry them well. Season with salt and pepper. Melt the butter in a pan and fry the bacon, onions and garlic until golden brown. Remove from the pan with a slotted spoon and place in a casserole. Add the rabbit joints and fry these for 5 minutes or until browned on all sides. Remove from the pan and place in the casserole. Stir the flour into the fat remaining in the pan and cook over a very gentle heat for about 10 minutes, stirring from time to time, until it becomes a rich brown colour. Gradually stir in the water and wine and bring to the boil, stirring all the time. Stir in the mustard and pour over the rabbit in the casserole. Add the mushrooms and thyme. Cover and cook in a moderate oven, 350°F, 180°C, Gas Mark 4 for 1½ hours. Taste and adjust the seasoning before serving. (Serves 4–6)

Vegetables and Salads

Lettuce with Butter and Thyme

1 crisp lettuce
juice of ½ lemon
pinch sugar
salt and freshly milled black pepper
2 teaspoons chopped thyme
3oz (75g/⅜ cup) butter

Wash the lettuce, dry well then tear into small pieces. Put into a serving bowl. Blend the lemon juice with the sugar, seasoning and thyme. Add to the lettuce and toss well. Just before serving, melt the butter and when it is hot and foaming pour over the lettuce. (Serves 4)

Courgettes (Zucchini) with Thyme

1lb (400g) courgettes
2oz (50g/¼ cup) butter
3 sprigs thyme
salt and freshly milled black pepper

Slice the courgettes (zucchini), but do not peel them. Melt the butter in a pan, add the courgettes (zucchini), thyme and seasoning. Shake the pan well, so that the courgettes (zucchini) do not stick to the bottom of the pan. Cover and cook over a gentle heat for about 15 minutes or until the vegetables are quite tender. Remove the thyme before serving. (Serves 4)

Gevulde Kool

Dutch Layered Cabbage

12 outer leaves from a cabbage, preferably a Savoy
salt
4 tablespoons oil
1 medium-sized onion, chopped
1 green pepper (capsicum), de-seeded and chopped
2oz (50g) mushrooms, sliced
8oz (200g) minced (ground) beef
8oz (200g) minced (ground) veal
2 tablespoons concentrated tomato purée
salt and pepper
2 teaspoons chopped thyme
1oz (25g/2 tablespoons) butter

Blanch the leaves in boiling salted water for 2 minutes, drain and dry well and put on one side. Heat the oil and fry the onion and green pepper (capsicum) for 5 minutes. Add the mushrooms, beef, veal, tomato purée, seasoning and thyme and cook for 5—8 minutes, stirring well.
Line a greased ovenproof dish with a layer of cabbage leaves. Spread with a layer of meat mixture. Cover with a layer of cabbage leaves and continue these layers, ending with a layer of cabbage. Dot with butter and bake in a moderately hot oven, 375°F, 190°C, Gas Mark 5 for 30—40 minutes until lightly browned. (Serves 4)

Fassoulia

8oz (200g/1⅓ cups) haricot (dried white) beans
¼ pint (125ml/⅝ cup) olive oil
1 large onion, chopped
2 cloves garlic, crushed
1 bay leaf
4 sprigs thyme
1 tablespoon concentrated tomato purée
juice of 1 lemon
salt and pepper
To Garnish:
2 tablespoons chopped parsley

Soak the haricot (dried white) beans in cold water overnight. Drain. Heat the oil in a pan and fry the onion for 10 minutes or until golden. Add the beans together with the garlic, bay leaf, thyme and tomato purée. Cook gently for 10 minutes then add sufficient boiling water to just cover the beans. Cover the pan and simmer gently for 2 hours or until the beans are quite tender. Add the lemon juice and season to taste. Allow the beans to cool in the liquid. When cold, turn into a serving dish and sprinkle with the chopped parsley before serving. (Serves 4)

Green Beans with Thyme

This recipe can be used for either French or runner beans.

1lb (400g) French or runner beans
salt
2oz (50g/¼ cup) butter
1 tablespoon olive oil
2 teaspoons chopped thyme
1 large clove garlic, crushed
freshly milled black pepper
1 tablespoon grated Parmesan cheese

Top, tail and string the beans and cut them into 2 inch (5cm) lengths. Cook in boiling salted water for 5 minutes, then drain well.
While the beans are cooking, heat the butter and oil in a saucepan, add the thyme and the garlic and cook gently for 5 minutes. Add the beans, toss well together and season with salt and pepper. Cook over a low heat, shaking the pan frequently for 5 minutes.
Add the Parmesan cheese, stir together then turn into a heated serving dish.

INDEX